Deadly Sins
And
Living Virtues

Living Beyond The Seven Deadly Sins

R. Curtis Fussell

CSS Publishing Company, Inc., Lima, Ohio

DEADLY SINS AND LIVING VIRTUES

Copyright © 1997 by
CSS Publishing Company, Inc.
Lima, Ohio

All rights reserved. No part of this publication may be reproduced in any manner whatsoever without the prior permission of the publisher, except in the case of brief quotations embodied in critical articles and reviews. Inquiries should be addressed to: Permissions, CSS Publishing Company, Inc., P.O. Box 4503, Lima, Ohio 45802-4503.

Scripture quotations are from the *Revised Standard Version of the Bible*, copyrighted 1946, 1952 ©, 1971, 1973, by the Division of Christian Education of the National Council of the Churches of Christ in the USA. Used by permission.

Library of Congress Cataloging-in-Publication Data

Fussell, R. Curtis, 1953-
  Deadly sins and living virtues : living beyond the seven deadly sins / R. Curtis Fussell.
      p.   cm.
  Includes bibliographical references.
  ISBN 0-7880-1138-3 (pbk.)
  1. Deadly sins—Sermons. 2. Sermons, American. I. Title.
BV4626.F87   1998
241'.3—dc21   97-26639
                                                                              CIP

This book is available in the following formats, listed by ISBN:
  0-7880-1138-3   Book
  0-7880-1139-1   IBM 3 1/2
  0-7880-1140-5   MAC
  0-7880-1141-3   Sermon Prep

PRINTED IN U.S.A.

*To Tempe Lee,
steadfast friend,
faithful companion,
and lovely wife;*

*And to our children,
Calee, Hannah, Rachel and Robert.*

Table Of Contents

Foreword   7

Deadly Sins:
A Matter Of Sutton's Law   9
   Romans 7:14-25

Pride:
An Occasion For Emptying   17
   Luke 18:9-14; Philippians 2:1-11

Envy:
Where Is The Grass Greener?   25
   Genesis 4; Matthew 20:1; Philippians 4:4-13

Anger:
Eleven Ways To Blow Up, Seven Ways To Cool Off   33
   Matthew 5:21-22; Romans 12:14-21; Ephesians 4:29-32

Sloth:
What Happens When Indifference Meets Enthusiasm?   41
   Matthew 25:14-30; Revelation 3:15-16

Lust:
To Discipline The Eye And The Heart   49
   Matthew 5:27-30; John 4:5-26

Greed:
Putting Things In Their Proper Perspective   57
   Matthew 6:25-34; 1 Timothy 6:6-10; Ecclesiastes 5:10-11

Gluttony:
Living by Bread And The Word Of God   67
   Mark 6:38-42; 1 Timothy 4:4-10

Foreword

These sermons were preached at Richlands Presbyterian Church, in Richlands, Virginia, during the eight weeks prior to Thanksgiving. This time was appropriate since Fall is the season for football games in which much pride, envy, and anger are expressed. Also, the final sermon on gluttony came the Sunday before Thanksgiving so that the congregation could, hopefully, belly up to the feast with some awareness that having food on the table does indeed mean living before God in the world.

These are sermons, not theological lectures that attempt to say everything that needs to be said about these topics. Their purpose is not just to interpret and explain, but to give form and provide substance for the ongoing effort to have life in Jesus Christ. In particular, I hope the reader will notice that I have not attempted to moralize the seven deadly sins, but rather to use them as signs, albeit rough and dangerous signs, pointing us in the direction of becoming better witnesses to the grace of God. If these sermons can do that, then I will be deeply pleased, for they will have done what they were intended to do.

Also allow me to say that as one who preaches every Sunday, and who has responsibility for the pastoral care of a congregation, I am constantly dependent on others to help me present the weekly sermons. Preaching is a shared art because it is simply impossible to find illustrations for and be original on every point. Preachers depend on the sermons of others to give insight as well as information. As the footnotes readily reveal, I heavily employed in the first three sermons many illustrations and points from Todd Jones, a classmate from seminary, who preached a similar series. Naturally though, while borrowing many of his items for my own backpack, we went separate ways. Also, I was helped by another series of sermons on the seven deadly sins preached by George Sinclair, who not only attended seminary with me, but has been a dear friend since our freshman days in college. I am indebted to both of these powerful preachers for insight and understanding on such difficult matters.

Gratitude is also extended to members at Richlands Presbyterian Church, who listened and responded to these sermons thoughtfully. Every one of these sins touches a nerve; hence one reason they are so deadly. They are not easy to talk about, not easy to preach, and not easy on the listener's ears. But the members at Richlands encouraged each week's message, showing me the support which every preacher needs in order to stand in the pulpit. Without the congregation's desire to hear, the preacher cannot preach.

Above all I am grateful to my wife Tempe, who is my closest neighbor, and whose insights, suggestions, and support have made my life, and not merely my ministry and these sermons, better and richer. And to our four children, Calee, Hannah, Rachel, and Robert, I also owe a word of gratitude for just being there to provide joyful distraction.

Curtis Fussell
Richlands, Virginia

Deadly Sins

A Matter Of Sutton's Law

Romans 7:14-25

You have said it before and I have, too, to a friend, your husband or wife: "I'm sorry. I didn't mean to say that. I'm just not myself today." And then maybe you have heard it said: "He's not really a bad boy; he's just trying to find himself." Or perhaps you have used this expression: "He's not human, he's an animal." Perhaps also you have said this about your boss: "He thinks he's God Almighty."[1]

All these expressions describe the contradiction that plagues all of us — that I am not, you are not, what we think we are. In the Bible it is called sin. Sin means we are not and we do not act as we should.

In the Middle Ages some men and women wanted to love God with all their heart, mind, and soul. So they reasoned that they first had to know the Word of God. But then they reasoned that they also needed to know the enemy; that which separated them from God. So they sought to describe sin as concretely as they could. Out of that desire to know the enemy arose a list of seven deadly sins: pride, envy, anger, sloth, greed, gluttony, and lust. And then it was said that out of these seven principal sins all other sins were connected. For instance, sloth entails malice. Anger leads to murder and cruelty. Greed is related to theft, and so forth.

We are going to be talking about sin over the next eight weeks. Not only because we are all plagued by these sins and made miserable by them, but because we want, like the medieval men and women, to know the enemy that spoils our lives. With this knowledge we may be better able to live in the image of Jesus Christ. Addressing these sins will, indeed, help us to see the enemy and then reveal to us what it takes to live the virtuous life as believers and followers of Jesus Christ. As it says in Proverbs, "Without a vision the people will perish" (29:18 KJV).

In talking about the seven deadly sins we are seeking above all to proclaim the Good News, the gospel of Jesus Christ. In talking about these seven deadly sins we are not saying God is a critical parent, snooping round to sniff out sins in order to punish or reject us. Instead our aim is to hear about these sins so we may come to name them, to make a confession about them, and then to repent, making it possible for us to turn away from them.

It will be tough going though. Our biggest danger will be our own self-deception. You see, all too easily we will think that one of these particular sins pertains especially to someone we have in mind, and not ourselves! But why? Because we prefer to think of ourselves not as sinners, but as nice people who occasionally run out of bounds and make mistakes.

Loren Eiseley, a naturalist, wrote a book called *The Immense Journey*[2] in which he describes an unforgettable event in his childhood. He and some friends were walking through a pastureland and discovered an old abandoned well. After removing the vines, they took the cover off to see down inside. At first all they could see was a deep, dark well, just enormous darkness, but in its midst they could also hear water trickling.

Suddenly, as they were peering into that deep darkness the clouds overhead moved and a shaft of sunlight lit up the bottom of the well. And there, on an old rusty pipe, Eiseley tells of seeing the ugliest, blackest, slimiest creature he had ever seen. As he remembered it, it had a thousand legs and horns all around its head. Scared to death at how hideous this creature was, Eiseley and his friends, as quickly as they could, put the top back on and ran away. Eiseley later reflected that only a creature that loved darkness could live in such conditions. Only a creature that wanted to live out of and get away from the light could live in such darkness.

But this scene is no less true of people. We are glad that there has been darkness to hide our sins. Even though there will come a time, as the apostle Paul says to the Corinthian church, when "the Lord will bring to light the things now hidden in darkness and will disclose the purposes of the heart" (1 Corinthians 4:5), for the moment, we are glad there's darkness.

Let me ask you a question. If someone took the lid off your life and looked down into its darkest parts, what would he find? What kind of ugliness would he see? If someone looked down into your deepest, darkest secrets, what kind of shameful thoughts would be exposed? What mean or totally embarrassing deed would be revealed? Imagine if we could get a video tape recorder and record your entire life; the unedited, uncensored, and unrated version of your life? Every thought you ever had, every word you ever spoke, every deed you did? And what if we were to show that tape here for everyone to see? Would you be willing to have such a showing with friends, neighbors, family, and church members all present? Let me ask, do we have any volunteers here for such a showing? Can I see a show of hands out there of those who are ready to show their unedited, unrated life? Is there anyone awake out there this morning?[3] (If someone does raise his hand, as a young person did in my congregation, you might say, "A brave person. I'm impressed that you would volunteer to undergo such an ordeal. The average person, the average church member, wouldn't dare.")

Quite naturally people avoid revealing their sins. It's quite normal to take actions, sometimes extraordinary actions, to avoid any of our sins being seen. But on occasion the deepest, darkest parts of who we are, are revealed. For instance, driving down the highway another car cuts in front of you, and suddenly things come out of your mouth that you never knew were there. Actions take place, anger boils out of you; and then you wonder, was that me? Where on earth did that come from? Was that really me? Well, you know what's happening. We would rather not admit it, but it's that dark side of us getting exposed to the light.[4]

It's a curious thing, but one of the most criticized parts of a Presbyterian worship service is the Confession of Sin. People say, "Why do we have to be reminded of all this negative stuff every week? It's just so negative, so gloomy, and right after a cheerful hymn of praise. Let's just talk about good things, positive things.

In church I don't want to be reminded of how wrong I am and how wrong the people around me are."

Such remarks, of course, point to the urge we all have to deny that we are sinners, the urge we all have to push away the dark side in us and pretend it isn't there. I hate to say it, but all of us — including myself — like to pretend we are better than we are. But no matter how hard we pretend and try to hide the dark side of us, something always comes up to expose our highly edited lives. Something always exposes the acts we use to fool others and even ourselves. Things come out of us; we do things and we can't imagine where they come from.

Embarrassed and hurt by these things, we suddenly find ourselves repeating the apostle Paul's words, "I do the things I do not want to do, and don't do the things I want to do; sin dwells within me" (Romans 7:15f). This thing in all of us, which the Bible calls sin, has a way of showing up sooner or later. Sin has a way of finding us no matter how hard we try to hide from it or pretend it isn't there.

Some may still say, "Yes, that may be true, but why do we have to talk about all this bad stuff? Why do we have to talk about sin? Can't we talk about something more uplifting in the church? There's a lot of good stuff out there and in here; it's unbalanced only to talk about sin." Well, the reason we talk about sin is because of Sutton's law. Sutton's law? Yes, it's a law named after Willie Sutton who was a famous bank robber. When Sutton was asked by a reporter why he robbed banks, he said, "Because that's where the money is." So the reason we focus on sin in church is because that's where the payoff is; that's where the wounds and pain are, and that, then, which is our real focus, is where healing can take place.[5]

Have you ever been to battle with pride, envy, anger, sloth, greed, gluttony, or lust? Of course you have, we all have. We battle with them, if not every day, then at least every week. But we want to deny these sins and say we have never really been attracted to them or even spent time with them. They're so unpleasant, frightening, and dangerous, and yet they are old acquaintances; we know them on a first name basis. We would call them old friends, if we called them friends. But they're the enemy.

Surprisingly, it is important, it is to our advantage, that we know these deadly sins on a first name basis because then we can deal with them by means of God's power. God's power to deal with sin comes to us in three ways: confession, repentance, and forgiveness.

Let's look at confessing our sins. In "Alcoholics Anonymous" three things are required. First of all you have to say, "I have a problem." No one else can make that statement, neither my wife, my husband, nor my parents. No, I alone am to blame for this problem. I am the problem. Second, you have to say, "I can't solve this problem alone, I need God's help." And third, you make a commitment to change, to turn away, to repent from the problem. To change your life. The Bible calls these three things by these names: confession, repentance, and forgiveness. These are the three things we use in dealing with the problem of sin. Wholeness and health come to us with the confession, "I did the thing I didn't want to do. I'm sorry. I am to blame."

Chris Webber, the star basketball player for the University of Michigan, managed to get ahold of the ball with only eleven seconds left in the final game of the 1993 NCAA tournament against the University of North Carolina. All he had to do was take the ball down the court, put the ball through the net, and Michigan would have won. But as Chris came down the court with the ball, he called for time-out. Unfortunately, his team had used up all their time-outs, and so they were penalized with a technical foul. UNC scored and won the game. After the game the reporters rushed Chris Webber, and his face was one of devastation.

He said this though, "I'm sorry. I lost the game. I apologize to my teammates." Chris Webber had made a mistake that brought him humiliation and loss, but he admitted it. He offered no excuses. He didn't say, "They should have told me!" He didn't say, "I'm only one player on the team, I'm not the only one who lost the game." He offered no excuses, but instead he apologized for his mistake. He said, "I lost the game, I made a mistake." A confession, straightforward and honest.[6]

Alice Metzenger lived in Oregon as a gourmet cook under that name for ten years. Then one day she went to the police and turned herself in for a crime she had committed 23 years earlier. A crime that would surely send her to prison. But Catherine Ann Howard, her real name, said she had to answer to that crime in the past to keep on living in the present. Her therapist said that this confession was bringing about healing in Catherine's life. Her husband said, "Catherine wants the truth and her life back. She wants to be whole again, and her confession is making that happen."[7]

Of course to confess your sins is no easy matter. To say, "I was wrong," takes enormous courage. But those few simple words can create a whole new world. Try using them some time. If you want to experience real power and healing in your life when you're trying to avoid guilt that really belongs to you, say it, "I was wrong," and then feel the burden being lifted and the surge of new life pouring in.

The second way to deal with sins is to repent from them. To repent means to make a U-turn, to turn away from those things that are not good and true. In the comic strip *Peanuts* Lucy is again trying to get Schroeder's attention as he plays the piano. Lucy asks, "Schroeder, what is love?" Schroeder stops playing the piano and replies, "Love is a strong attachment to someone, loyalty to someone or something, devotion to a person or persons." Then Schroeder goes back to playing the piano, and Lucy responds, "My, doesn't he look great on paper?"[8]

Indeed, the highly edited version of our lives that we present to others looks great on paper, but things aren't what they seem. I know how that happens with me. There have been times when my wife has reviewed one of my sermons, and then she makes the comment, "Great sermon, too bad you don't live it."[9] My response has been, "Now come on, wait a minute." But it's true. We can talk the talk, we can know what's right and good and true, look great on paper, but do we live it?

Sigmund Freud once said, "I have found little that is good about human beings; in my experience most of them are trash."[10] I think Jesus would reply to Dr. Freud by saying, "What you overlook, Dr. Freud, is that human beings can be recycled, people can change;

a person, no matter how trashed his life is, can be born again into a new person by deciding to turn and follow me." People can repent of their sins. As we say in church, people can be born again.

The third way the Bible deals with sin is to proclaim the forgiveness of God. Young children inevitably will hurt themselves. They stumble over their shoes and fall on the hard pavement, skinning their knees. They pinch their fingers playing with clothespins.

There are adults who have hurt themselves and others in worse ways by the actions they have committed. Anyone devastated by the losses resulting from words and actions may well wonder, "Can I ever be restored? Can there ever be healing? Preacher, you have no idea how hurt I am, how messed up my life is. Can I ever be restored?"

What I say is this: "Yes. Yes. Yes." Yes, you can be restored. Because where there is pain, agony, loss, brokenness and shame there is above all of that God's grace in Jesus Christ. By God's grace we can be made whole and healthy again. By God's grace we can have new life and become a new person, because by God's grace we receive the good news that our sins are forgiven and washed away by the body, the blood, and the resurrection of Jesus Christ. Come now to this memorial table set with signs of the death and resurrection of Jesus, and be born again into a new person through the grace of God in Jesus Christ, who forgives us our sins, calls us to live before God, and gives us new life.

Children's Message

For an object use a dry eraser pen and board. Ask the children about things they have done that they knew were wrong; *e.g.*, using bad language, hitting, yelling. Write these actions on the board, but as you write the words misspell them. Then talk to the children about how we are here in church to learn and know how we can stop doing those kinds of things that hurt others and ourselves. Remind the children that "Jesus calls us to do good. But of course sometimes we make mistakes. See, look at these words. I misspelled every one of them! Now, what do you do when you misspell words? Yes, you erase them and start over. *(Erase the words.)* So here's an example of the good news we have in Jesus Christ. First, we see that we make mistakes. Then, we do something to correct those mistakes. We tell someone we are sorry. Or we go and make things right. And when we do that, it makes us feel so good. God does the same thing with us. In Jesus Christ, God hears us when we say we're sorry and then wipes away our mistakes so we can start over again. And it makes us feel so good; like we are brand-new."

---

1. Shirley C. Guthrie, *Christian Doctrine*, Rev. ed. (Westminster/John Knox Press: Louisville, KY, 1994), p. 212.

2. Loren Eiseley, *The Immense Journey* (Random House: New York, NY, 1959), pp. 37-38.

3. Adapted from the audiotape sermon series by Todd Jones, *An Album of Sermons on "The Seven Deadly Sins"* (First Presbyterian Church, 393 E. Main Street, Spartanburg, SC 29302), tape number 1, "The Deadly Sins" (1994).

4. Adapted from Jones, *ibid.*

5. Scott Peck, *Further Along the Road Less Traveled: The Unending Journey Toward Spiritual Growth* (Simon and Schuster: New York, NY, 1993), p. 45.

6. "I Cost Our Team the Game," by William F. Reed in *Sports Illustrated*, Vol. 78, April 1993, p. 28ff; adapted from Jones, *ibid.*

7. Adapted from Jones, *ibid.*

8. Jones, *ibid.*

9. *Ibid.*

10. Cited by Robert Wolff in *About Philosophy*, 5th edition (Prentice-Hall: Englewood Cliffs, NJ, 1992), p. 284.

Pride

An Occasion For Emptying

Luke 18:9-14; Philippians 2:1-11

Girolamo Savonarola was one of the great preachers of the fifteenth century. He preached in the great cathedral of Florence, Italy, which contained a magnificent marble statue of the blessed virgin Mary. When Savonarola started preaching at this great cathedral, he noticed one day an elderly woman praying before this statue of Mary. He then began to notice that it was her habit to come every day and pray before the statue.

Savonarola remarked one day to an elderly priest who had been serving in the cathedral for many years, "Look how devoted and earnest this woman is. Every day she comes and offers prayers to the blessed Mother of Jesus. What a marvelous act of faith." But the elderly priest replied, "Do not be deceived by what you see. Many years ago when the sculptor needed a model to pose for this statue of the blessed Mother, he hired a beautiful young woman to sit for him. This devout worshiper you see here everyday is that young woman. She is worshiping who she used to be."[1]

The first and perhaps the deadliest of the seven deadly sins is pride. The *Oxford Dictionary* defines pride as an "unduly high opinion of one's own qualities, merits, that is, an arrogant bearing." In other words, pride is self-love that says, "I'm better than you." You see pride in others when someone makes a boast of his or her accomplishment as though you are expected to pay homage.

Muhammad Ali had just won another boxing title. On the airplane the stewardess politely said to him, "You need to fasten your seat belt." Ali replied, "Superman doesn't need a seat belt." To which the stewardess politely responded, "And Superman doesn't need an airplane either; please fasten your seat belt."[2]

You see pride when a parent or grandparent talks endlessly about what Johnny has done as though he were a wonder child and you should marvel at his presence and activities. We live in an age when parents are attentive to their children, constantly praising them, in part to encourage their self-esteem. In fact, this encouragement can lead children to be overachievers, or cause them to think of themselves as better than anyone else. We may never know how many children have been psychologically and emotionally damaged because their parents pushed them to be outstanding based on pride.

You also see pride in Christians who quote Bible passages, not in an effort to help others gain spiritual wisdom, but to show others how much they know. Quoting the Bible can be a put-down, a display of triumphant pride.

But we see pride best in ourselves. When we become irritated at someone who has corrected us, and we hear ourselves saying, "Who does he think he is correcting me?" — that's pride. Or when we are offended because we don't get the kind of recognition we think we deserve — that's pride. Or there on the car bumper a sticker that says: "My child is an honor roll student at Academic High School" — that's pride. Of course, there's another kind of pride which was displayed on the bumper of a pickup truck that said, "My child beat up your honor roll student."

Of course, not all pride is bad. It's good to take pride in our churches, our schools, our communities, and even in ourselves. That is, pride is good when we are striving to make life better for everyone. Pride as self-worth is important and necessary because it lets us see ourselves as having gifts that can make life better for everyone around us.

But it is the sin of pride that damages; and pride becomes a sin when we talk and act in a way that says, "I'm better than you." That kind of pride is a sin. In a manner of speaking, pride is like the tires on your car. The tires don't function right if they are underinflated or overinflated.[3] Neither way is good for the tire. Like automobile tires, it is important for us not to be underinflated or overinflated in our opinion about ourselves. But unfortunately, while many people suffer from low self-esteem, most people have the tendency to overinflate themselves.

Evidence for an overinflated opinion of ourselves comes from the College Board that administers the Scholastic Aptitude Test, the SAT exam, which millions of high school students take each year. On that test there are a number of other questions besides the ones about math and English which the students are asked to answer. For instance, they are asked to evaluate their leadership ability.

Recently in an exam, seventy percent of the students rated themselves as above average in leadership, and only two percent as below average. Sixty percent rated themselves as above average in athletics while only six percent said below. When they rated themselves as to how easy they were to get along with, 25 percent said they were in the top one percent, sixty percent said they were in the top ten percent, and absolutely no one said he was below average in being easy to get along with.

Obviously high school students have a very high opinion of themselves; they have pride in themselves. Now is this the kind of pride that says, "I have something to offer this world to make it a better place," or is it the kind of pride that says, "I'm better than you"? The exam doesn't say. We hope it's pride that offers to build a better world; otherwise, it is arrogance.

Perhaps arrogance is the best description of the sin of pride. Normally when we talk about sin, we usually think of mistakes we have made, bad judgment, weak character so that we gave in to temptation. Sin, in fact, is commonly thought by many people to be a weakness in character, a character flaw. But pride can only be described as a sin of strength. It says, "I'm somebody"; it says, "I have more than you, I'm better than you; I deserve special recognition."

The apostle Paul though said, "Have this mind among yourselves, in humility count others better than yourselves." It seems that in the church in Philippi there were members who were trying to set themselves up as better than others. Who knows what it was, maybe, "I'm more spiritual than you," or "I know the Bible better than you do." Or "I've worked and served this church for more than twenty years, don't I deserve some recognition?"

But Paul reminds them to count others better than themselves because our Lord and Savior Jesus Christ, even though he was equal with God in his very being, emptied himself for others, so we could have life. That's the model then — not to be high and mighty, but to be open and receptive, to be empty so as to allow others to come in, rather than so full of yourself that there's no room for anyone else.

A city boy visited his cousin who lived on a farm in the country for the first time. The city boy had never seen wheat growing in a field. It was an impressive sight for him, the wheat golden brown and ready for harvesting. He noticed that some of the wheat stood tall in the field, whereas some of it was bent low, touching the ground. The city boy said to his cousin, "I bet the ones standing tall are the best ones, aren't they?" His cousin smiled knowingly and reached over and plucked the head of one of the tall-standing wheat stalks and one that was bent to the ground. He rubbed each of them and the city boy saw that the tall one was almost empty of seeds. But the one bent to the ground was full of the promise of a rich harvest.[4]

Someone has said we would do well to wear our talents like a pocket watch — to keep them hidden and only pull them out when someone is in need.

Jesus tells the story of two men who went to the Temple to worship God, a Pharisee and a tax collector. The Pharisee was a model of faith. He worshiped regularly, served as an elder and teacher in the church; he was a devoted husband, he was honest in all his business practices. He tithed his earnings to the church. Here was a man who was everything we want in being a faithful follower of God, a model of faith for our children and even us adults. But his heart was full of pride. He prayed, "God, I thank you that I am not like other people." A sign outside a church captures this scene: "If you look down on others, then how can you look up to God?" It is a contradiction. You see, if God wanted us to pat ourselves on the back, don't you think God would have given us joints to make it easy to do? This Pharisee was so full of himself, so utterly full of himself. But all of us know how easy it is to become full of ourselves, to think that we have done something worthy to be counted better than others.

At work we think we work harder than others, so we deserve a raise or special consideration. In our marriages we believe we give more to the relationship; my wife, my husband, should appreciate me more.

The sin of pride is to think we are better than others. I was proud when I was given the trophy in the ninth grade for the Most Valuable Player on the football team. I was proud when I was voted the best athlete in junior high school. I was proud when I won a gold medal in the Junior Olympics. I was proud when I was elected senior class president. I was proud when I graduated from college and three years later from seminary. I was proud when I received my Doctor of Ministry and then my Ph.D. I know about pride, about counting myself better than others.

Fortunately though, I have a wife, four children, and this congregation to remind me that I'm not Superman, that I don't know everything, that indeed I make mistakes and that only by the grace of God do I know success of any kind.

A martial arts student was meeting with his master and teacher at a table, having tea. The student said to his master, "I've learned all you have to teach me about defending myself. I want to learn one thing more now. Please teach me about the ways of God."

The master took the teakettle and starting pouring the student's cup full of tea. Soon the cup was full and began to spill over onto the saucer. But the master continued to pour the tea until it spilled over the saucer and then onto the floor.

The student finally said, "Stop, stop, the tea is spilling over. The cup can't take any more." The master then looked at the student and said, "You are so full of yourself that there is no room in your life for God. It is not possible for you to learn the ways of God until you learn to empty yourself."[5]

That's what the apostle Paul says to us. If you want to learn the ways of God, then listen to this: Jesus Christ had the very nature of God, but he did not count himself too good or as deserving special treatment and recognition. No, he emptied himself and became a servant, serving even the likes of you and me; and even dying for you and me. We call that humility. Jesus Christ humbled himself, gave himself, so we might have life. It wasn't pride in who he was as the Son of God that had the power of redemption. No, it was his humiliation that had the power to make things new.

A little girl at the circus bought a huge cone of cotton candy. A man passing by said to her, "How can a little girl like you eat so much cotton candy?" She replied, "Well, Mister, I'm really bigger on the inside than on the outside."

Do you want to be bigger on the inside than you are on the outside? Do you want to be humble, to give life, to make life fuller? Then have this mind among yourselves: "I have been given much, not so that I might be better than others, but that I might share even that which I have."

Children's Message

When you think of a teddy bear you think of a fuzzy animal with arms sticking out. Have you ever seen a teddy bear with his arms crossed and a frown on his face? I haven't! But maybe you have seen a person cross his arms. Maybe you've seen a friend with crossed arms in front of you, who says in a rough voice, "I don't want to play with you!" Then maybe that person turned around, stomped his feet, and walked away. How does that make you feel? Not good! No, it hurts. Sometimes friends, and even you and I, act in ways like that, when we think we're too good to play or be with someone else. Well, listen to this very carefully: Jesus never thought he was too good for anybody. No, indeed; Jesus always has his arms open to you when you are looking for him. You can trust Jesus to have his arms open to you whenever you are looking for him, no matter where you are, no matter what you've done, because Jesus said, "Come to me." As good and wonderful as Jesus was, he never thought he was too good to turn away from someone who wanted him. Anyone who comes to Jesus, anyone who looks for Jesus, he will receive him or her with open arms and a warm, friendly smile. And so Jesus is an example to us, to love others as we love ourselves.

1. Adapted from Jones, *op. cit.*, tape number 6.

2. Jones, *ibid.*

3. *Ibid.*

4. *Ibid.*

5. Adapted from "Full to the Top," in *Stories for the Journey: A Sourcebook for Christian Storytellers*, by William R. White (Augsburg Press: Minneapolis, MN, 1988), p. 63.

Envy

Where Is The Grass Greener?

Genesis 4; Matthew 20:1; Philippians 4:4-13

I have a friend by the name of Robert who has always enjoyed playing jokes, especially at the expense of others. One day Robert was expecting a visit from his childhood friend Larry, whom he hadn't seen in over ten years. In their teens Robert and Larry had a friendly rivalry going between them. So Robert came up with this idea of trying to impress Larry that he had become extremely wealthy. There was a very exclusive neighborhood in town with many magnificent homes which would be ideal for this scheme. Robert had talked about this scheme with his buddies at the Lions' Club. As it happened, one of the Lion members who lived in this neighborhood offered Robert his home for a couple hours the day of Larry's arrival to pull off the deception. The owner said, "Here are the keys, just drive up to the house, go in, and make yourself at home. Get some refreshments out of the refrigerator. And then after a while, we'll let Larry in on the joke."

So the day came when Larry came to town. Robert picked him up at the airport in a fancy rented car. Then Robert drove Larry to the mansion. Indeed it was a magnificent house, made of grey stone with a tree-lined driveway. They drove up to the front door, walked into the house, found the den and refrigerator. Suddenly, though, as they were relaxing and talking, a man came into the room looking shocked and angry. He said, "What on earth are you doing in my house? Get out of here at once or I'll call the police!" And Robert said, "But Dave Butler knows we're here." But the man replied, "So what? Dave Butler lives in the house next door, not here!"[1]

That's a humorous conclusion to an act of envy. But envy is anything but humorous. Some people are said to be "consumed by envy," which aptly expresses the pain, the suffering, and the obsession that can come from being envious of another person.

It's important though not to confuse envy with jealousy. Jealousy is having something and fearing that you will lose it.[2] Also, envy can be confused with admiration. Someone can say he is envious of a pro golfer's swing, meaning he sees the benefit of it and wants to imitate it for his own benefit.

But envy is different because envy has a dark side to it. Envy is that feeling or that impression that someone else has something that is better than what you have. Envy is that feeling that you are inferior, that you are lacking something. So envy is saying, "I want what you have, because what you have is better than what I have."

The root of envy is comparing yourself to others. Its ugly head rises up when you think someone else is smarter, stronger, richer, or more beautiful than you are, has something better than you have, and suddenly you find yourself craving this thing that you think will make your life better. You become resentful that the other person has it, and that resentment is envy.

Of course, we are all susceptible to envy. Remember playing the game, "If only"? "If only I were married to that person. If only I had that job. If only I had that home. If only I had his talents, or her looks. If only I had their money. If only I had ... I mean, if I only had that ... my life would be so much better."[3]

Why do we envy? Why do we resent the success of our brothers and sisters, our friends and neighbors? His son makes the team; her daughter becomes a cheerleader, and all we see is red.

Why do we envy? Why do we doubt our own achievements and talents? "I don't like my life. Your life looks better. Let's trade. Because if I only had ... if I only had that ... well, then my life would be so much better." Really?

That must have been what Cain was saying about his brother Abel. "If only my offering were better, then God would love me more!" Really, Cain? This is a story about envy told about a brother problem, which means it involves a God problem. It is a God problem because as Genesis says, "God had regard for Abel and his offering, but not for Cain and his offering" (Genesis 4:5).

Some have tried to blame Cain himself for God's rejection. They say Cain didn't give the first and best fruit, that what Cain offered was small and stingy. But the Bible doesn't say that. It says in fact that Cain gave God an offering from the fruit of the ground. Cain gave what he could, what he had to offer, just as Abel did.

Others have then said it is really not a story about envy, nor sibling rivalry, nor God; no, it is a story that says that the Israelites as shepherds are better people than farmers. But the Bible doesn't say that either.

No, what the story says is that indeed life is not equal. Some people do have more than others. Some people do in fact do things better than others, better than you or I can do them. But God says to Cain, and to you and me who experience other people having advantages over us, "Listen, if you do well, you will be accepted." God says, "Listen, Cain. Listen, everybody: everyone has talents, gifts, duties, responsibilities. If you do well, you will be accepted. There is no excuse for comparing yourself with others. Make use of what has been given to you, because you know you are accepted."

Unfortunately Cain didn't listen. He rose up and killed his brother Abel. The sin of envy is deadly because it insists on making the playing field level. Now we may not go out and literally kill the person we envy; but then character assassination and dirty gossip are familiar techniques for "getting even," for putting down someone we envy, someone we think is better or has more than we do.

A man sells his business and pockets several million dollars. Someone says, "Roger has all that money, but he spends it only on himself. If I had millions, I would share it with the entire family, support charitable causes in all kinds of places. My money would help people. But Roger doesn't do any of that, he's so greedy and selfish." Envy reduces us to assassinating someone's character. Roger may have more money, but we can argue that we are morally superior. We feel there's a balance; envy has leveled the field.

It is amazing, when you begin to look for it, what a central role envy plays in the Bible. Do you realize that it was envy that caused Adam and Eve to be cast out of paradise? They wanted to be like God! Level the playing field. They wanted to have knowledge of good and evil. Why? Because they didn't have it; they wanted to be like God. There they were in Paradise, and yet it wasn't enough for Adam and Eve. "Count your blessings, one by one." "Oh, no, I want what you have, God, and then life will be better." They took the forbidden fruit, and sin and death entered the world, all because of envy.

You had better be careful with envy because it's still deadly stuff. A postal worker in Dearborn, Michigan, lost a job promotion to a fellow worker. He became so enraged with envy that he took a gun and shot this fellow worker twice in the head and then turned the gun on himself. There is the so-called "Pom Pom Mom" in Texas. Her daughter was not selected to be on the high school cheerleading team. This mother put out a contract to have the girl murdered whom she identified as the one who took her daughter's place. Fortunately this murder plot was found out. But what a monster envy had created.

Envy rises up in us and if we don't deal with it, we can say, "I so much want to have what you have that I'll do anything to make it mine." None of us has allowed envy to go to the extreme as it did with the postal worker or the Pom Pom Mom, but all of us have grudgingly envied someone at some time in our lives.

The classic case is the envy between brothers and sisters. A woman had a sister sixteen years younger than her. Obviously Mom and Dad raised these two girls differently. In the period between the birth of the two girls the parents had changed and times had changed in the way these sisters were raised. For instance, the elder one didn't get a car when she went off to college, but her younger sister did. There were lots of other little things that Mom and Dad did and gave to the younger daughter that made the elder daughter think, "Mom and Dad treated you better than me." But one day the younger daughter came to her older sister and asked her, "Did Mom do this with you? Did Dad do that with you?" And the older sister said, "Yes, we had a marvelous time." And the younger sister responded, "They never did that with me. I guess they were too busy for me. I wish I had been born first." To the older sister's amazement she suddenly realized that they both had been envious of each other for years, and for no good reason at all. It was all just a matter of a different time, and different people, and not a matter of some advantage one had over the other. They were both loved by their parents, and they were both lovely people.

Envy seems to be a given in growing up. Children envy other children's toys. I remember very clearly when I was eight years old envying a ten-speed bicycle my friend got for Christmas. I only had a three-speed. I was envious. And so I didn't like to go bicycling with my friend. But if I did, I would pedal like crazy to show him that my three-speed bike was as good as any ten-speed bike.

Teenagers envy their friends and schoolmates. They envy one another's looks, clothes, academic ability, athletic abilities; they envy their cars and their popularity. Then when these teens grow up to become adults, they envy one another's position, job, home, personality. By the time they become older people in retirement years, you would think that people would have come to accept and value themselves. But even for older people envy is a force to reckon with.

I was visiting Alice in the nursing home. Alice was in her mid-eighties. It was obvious when she came to the door that she was steamed about something. I said, "Alice, what's the matter?"

And she said, "It's that no good Doris."

I said, "Alice, wait a minute, I know Doris. What are you talking about?"

"Did you see that new furniture on her porch?"

"No, as a matter of fact I hadn't noticed it."

"You're just being nice. But Doris bought that furniture just to show me up. But I'll show her. I'm going shopping this weekend and I'll buy something that will let Doris know that she can't show me up."[4]

At every age we are susceptible to envy. We never seem to outgrow our capacity to focus on what someone else has. We remain blind to the gifts and blessings that are ours.

Let me suggest that there are three stages[5] in the cycle of envy. The first stage says that the grass is greener on the other side of the fence. At this stage we feel inferior and resent, if not hate, the other person. That was the stage where Alice was at. Instead of appreciating what was hers and who she was, she grumbled that someone else had an advantage. "Abel, let's take a walk in the field." The grass is greener on the other side.

The second stage is to say that the grass is indeed greener on the other side, but then notice too that it needs mowing. Here you may envy someone else, but then realize that, "Hey, it's not all sparkle. Maybe they don't have it as good as I think they do." I heard someone say once, "I envy the President of the United States. He's a world leader, a history maker. But I wouldn't have his job. I mean all the criticism he gets, all the headaches and problems he has to deal with. I envy the position, but I wouldn't have his job."

The third stage is to say, "Hey, you know the grass is green on the other side, but the grass is really nice on my side of the fence, too." Yes, it looks very green on the other side, but I have a lovely family, and I do like my job even though it is sometimes a pain in the neck. I'm content with my looks, my gifts; in fact I'm content with my whole life. It's a wonderful life! Stage three says, "Thank you, God, for allowing me to enjoy all that I have been given. I'm content and I see that my life is full of riches from you. The grass is really nice on my side of the fence."

He was a young man when he inherited the farm. Though it gave him a decent living, after many years he became discontent with it, tired of it. He felt chained to the farm. Others seemed to have more freedom. He began to feel he needed a change. It was about that time that he began to find all kinds of things wrong with the farm. Little things, annoyances here and there. He finally came to the conclusion that he wanted to sell the farm.

So he called a realtor who came out to the farm and looked it over. The realtor decided an advertised description of the farm placed in the newspaper would sell it quickly. He wrote this description: "A lovely working farm for sale. Ideal setting, picturesque location. Wooded acreage with large hardwoods. Well kept, healthy livestock, fertile land."

Before the realtor put this description in the newspaper, he let the farmer read it to make sure it was in order. The farmer read the advertisement; but after a little reflection he turned to the realtor and said, "This may sound crazy, but I'll take that farm. It's exactly what I've wanted all my life."[6]

We often forget or overlook the blessings that are ours. Do you realize that there are countless others who can only dream of the blessings you enjoy? We complain and say, "Oh, my life would be so much better if only I had what he has." A man who lived in a middle-class neighborhood made it a practice to take his children to the poor neighborhoods of the city. He did it to give his children a sense of the suffering of people and to instill in his children a sense of compassion and social responsibility. But one of the results that came from those visits was that when his children were older they appreciated what they had in life. As adults, because of that experience, they were far less prone to envy what others had.[7]

Take stock today and this week of the envious feelings you have. Think about them in light of all the blessings you enjoy. You will then learn to put off envy and be content with the life God has given you. Hopefully you will learn to say with the apostle Paul, "I have learned in whatever state I am, to be content ... because I know that if I do well, I am accepted." Jesus describes this attitude as being blessed with a poor spirit: "Blessed are the poor in spirit." You see, those with a poor spirit are ones who have an unassuming dignity and peace with themselves. They have seen the value of who they are and their station in life, because they have received the value with which God values them, given in the person and work of Jesus Christ.

Children's Message

Ask the children if they know of anyone who is perfect. "Do you know someone who makes all A's in school, someone who is an outstanding athlete, someone with a wonderful personality, good looks, and fine clothes? Have you ever wanted to be like someone else because you thought he or she was better than you? *(At this point show a hand-painted cup with flaws, e.g., cracks, chips, etc.)* Look at this cup. Pretty, isn't it? But if you look closely you will see some flaws, some cracks. Even this beautiful cup isn't perfect; but it's still beautiful. Well, let me tell you that no one, no matter how good he or she looks, is perfect. Everyone has something wrong. Everyone wishes he or she could do something better or be a better person. And everyone wants to be a special person. We all want other people to think the best of us because we know, even if we are not the best at everything, there are some very special things about each one of us.

"So I want to tell you to think about this: God has made you a very special person, too. You are special in your own way with all kinds of wonderful talents and abilities. And above all, you have heard it said, and it's true, that God loves you. Will you say this after me: God loves me. I'm a special person. And life is good because God loves me."

---

1. Adapted from Todd Jones, *op. cit.*, tape number 3.

2. Solomon Schimmel, *The Deadly Sins: Jewish, Christian and Classical Reflection on Human Nature* (Free Press: New York, NY, 1992), p. 80.

3. Jones, *ibid.*

4. Adapted from Jones, *ibid.*

5. These three stages are drawn from Jones, *ibid.*

6. Jones, *ibid.*

7. Schimmel, *ibid.*, p. 59.

Anger
Eleven Ways To Blow Up, Seven Ways To Cool Off

Matthew 5:21-22; Romans 12:14-21; Ephesians 4:29-32

What is your AQ? Not your IQ, which is your so-called intelligence quotient, but your AQ, your Anger Quota? Everyone has an AQ. Everyone has a point, a threshold, whatever you call it. If the right buttons are hit, you will get angry and start to growl, and that's your AQ, your Anger Quota. Of course, you and the people sitting around you don't look like you could be angry. As far as you and I can tell, everyone here looks calm, relaxed, quiet, and composed.

But under that cool composure there's the capacity to show anger. In some of us that anger is right now close to 212 degrees Fahrenheit — the boiling point. At any moment, someone could say just a word, do some little thing, and you would start growling or maybe even blow up like a volcano, spewing out venomous anger in all directions. So what is your AQ, your Anger Quota? Just for fun, let me give you a test. I promise I won't ask any of you to reveal your test scores.[1]

Imagine yourself approaching the express checkout line at the grocery store. The sign clearly says, "Twelve Items Or Less." Now you've counted the number of items in your basket. You have eight items. You naturally expect everyone else who gets in the express line to have twelve or fewer items, as you have.

But if you are expecting to find a cheater who will get in that express line just to get quicker service, you're a prime candidate for an episode of anger. In fact, this is the first stage of anger: you expect to be made angry. You are looking for something bad to happen; you are looking for the negative.

Now then, you approach the express line. And there in front of you is a guy with more than twelve items. It's obvious he has more than twelve items; his basket is full. Will your pulse rate start to rise? Will you feel that your territory has been violated? Will you feel yourself wanting to say, "Hey, he's taking advantage of the system?" If so, then you have entered stage two of anger. You have an evil eye set on the person. You are angry. Yet most people will just ride out this wave of anger. Most people will grumble to themselves and sit on this kind of anger. Of course, you may express a friendly smile toward the cheater, but behind that smile you will have derogatory thoughts about this express line cheater; and yet you will keep quiet and try not to show your anger. This is stage two of anger.

But if things are just right, if you have had other aggravating things happen at the office, or at home, if your blood is already 210 degrees Fahrenheit, you may not be able to keep quiet. You are ready to take off. And there, suddenly, you find yourself leaning over and saying something nasty to that express line cheater: "Hey, do you mind — you have more than twelve items. Who do you think you are?"

Congratulations, you've hit stage three. Does it feel good? Well, maybe for an instant when you let off the steam. But deep down it is a painful experience. Getting angry, losing your cool, yelling, screaming, and cursing someone is a painful experience.[2]

It is also an unhealthy experience. According to Dr. Radford Williams, a Duke University researcher, all three stages of anger damage your health, but in particular stage three. One study of anger in young men concluded that if they were prone to outbreaks of anger, they were seven times more likely to have heart disease or die by the age of fifty. In other words, anger kills. Anger is deadly.[3]

Anger is scary stuff, too. It is frightening to find yourself losing your temper or facing someone who is angry. As scary and painful as anger is though, you cannot ignore it, you can't pretend it doesn't exist, or that you never let it take hold of you. But then neither can we just let anger run wild. Anger has to be managed.

I suspect that many of you have in fact come here this morning seeking to manage your anger. In fact there are some, to speak tongue in cheek, who even want to manage their life with more anger and misery than they already have. What I want to do is show you eleven ways to ensure that you keep yourself in a state of uproar and anger. These eleven ways to make yourself good and angry come from the psychologist Les Carter in his book on anger.[4] But be careful. The tendency on hearing these methods is to say "I hope so-and-so heard that. That's exactly how he acts." No, the point here is, when and where do you act like this?

1. If you want to be angry, **take pride in being a perfectionist** and expect perfection in everyone else. Be a picky person; make it a habit. Live with the conviction that you can mold and change the people around you. Make it a point to force people around you into doing what you know they should and ought to do. And make sure to be furious with anyone who makes a mistake, who does not do things in a proper manner and put things in their proper place. As a perfectionist be sure to fuss loudly about bills and letters misplaced, typewriter mistakes, late appointments. You will hit the boiling point in no time and help others hit the mark quickly, too.

2. If you want to be angry, **don't listen to anyone else's view** but keep pushing your own. No one else in the world knows as much as you do. Always believe that your way is the best way. State your view often and preferably with a great deal of volume.

3. If you want to be miserable, **overload your schedule**. Make yourself so busy that you are always on edge, ensuring that you are like a rubber band stretched and always ready to snap at the slightest little thing.

4. If you want to be angry, **expect other people to cater to your needs**. After all, that's why God put other people in the world, isn't it, to serve your needs, to heed your complaints?

5. If you want to be angry, **never laugh and have a good time**, never be easygoing, because life is very serious business. Everything you say and do is of profound wisdom and utter importance.

6. If you want to be miserable, **have no compassion for others**. Show no concern for the poor and the jobless. After all, you achieved your position in life by your own hard work and diligence, let the poor do the same. Forget that the Bible talks about helping others and showing compassion, you just keep on saying, "It's their own fault. God helps those who help themselves."

7. If you want to be miserable, **make fun of and put down people who are different from you**. If someone else is from a different tradition, a different country, has a different skin color, and is from a different culture, be sure to talk ugly about him, using words carefully chosen to ensure that the person is looked down on.

8. If you want to be angry, **practice shouting**. No matter that common sense tells you that a quiet voice brings about understanding and harmony. Since your goal in life is to be miserable, when others don't see and do things the way you do, start shouting and yelling at them. This is particularly effective for creating miserable homes in which to live.

9. If you want to be angry, **worship money and possessions**. Remember, it is the almighty dollar that demands your time and talent. Always seek to make more money than your brother, your sister, and your friends. Be outrageously envious of the money and things they have. And, of course, always use people in whatever way you can to gain all the money and possessions you worship.

10. If you want to be angry, **never pay any attention to your own faults and weaknesses**. Focus instead on the faults and weaknesses of others. **And above all learn to be offended at any remarks and corrections that are directed your way.** Naturally this means you must never read the Bible because it could highlight some changes in your own life which might bring you peace of mind.

11. If you want to be angry, **learn to nag, learn to nitpick, practice criticism and the snide remark.** Learn and practice that fine art of pointing out what's wrong with other people. Be sure to point out those faults in a public place so everyone else can see that you mean business. If you don't point out others' faults, who is going to do that for them?

There you have it, eleven ways to a life of misery, rage, and anger of all kinds, for yourself and everyone around you.

Turn now and look at what the Bible says about anger. Anger is no stranger to the Bible. By the fourth chapter of Genesis, the first family suffers the deadly effects of anger when Cain kills his brother Abel in a rage of anger. Moses goes into a fit of anger when he comes down from Mount Sinai with the tablets of the law and finds the Israelites worshiping an idol. Moses smashes the tablets, grinds up the golden calf into powder, and force-feeds it to the idol worshippers, who are then slaughtered. Moses was angry!

Of course, by far the most angry person in the Old Testament — are you ready for this? The most angry person in the Bible is God. Again and again you read the words, "the anger of the Lord was kindled against Israel." It was God's anger that brought the Great Flood. God was angry when Job asked him, "Why?" It was the anger of God that brought the Babylonians to Israel where they destroyed the Temple. Almost one third of the Psalms refer in some way to the anger of God; the Psalmists are found offering prayers imploring God to turn away from wrath and anger.

In the New Testament Jesus showed anger at the money changers in the temple, overturning their tables and driving them out. Jesus was angry with the Pharisees who watched to see whether he would heal someone on the Sabbath. Mark says Jesus was grieved at the hardness of their hearts and looked around at them with anger. Jesus expressed anger toward Peter when he shot back, "Get behind me, Satan. Your way is not the way of God." Jesus was angry!

The apostle Paul was angered by some preachers in Galatia who were demanding the Gentiles to be circumcised. In an outburst of anger, Paul said he hoped they would mutilate themselves. Paul was angry!

All these examples of anger in the Bible are negative ones. But the Bible also shows that anger is not always negative, not always bad. Anger can be positive and have a rightful place in life. As the examples show, God, Jesus, and Paul are angry at evil, at false worship of God, at what distorts the good news. The Bible speaks of God hating evil and loving good. As one prayer goes, "God, let me love what you love and hate what you hate." The thing though is to avoid becoming a negative, destructive hater.

Anger. I don't think there's any doubt about it, anger is the most common and the most destructive emotion there is. Contrary to popular opinion, love is certainly not the most common emotion. There are people so consumed by anger that not a ray of love penetrates their mantel. You can even see it on their faces, that frowning, haggard look. I remember the face of a man I knew who was consumed by anger. There was a darkness about his face, an edginess in his looks, with his shoulders bent down in rage. He had spent years fighting for the rights of poor and oppressed people, and it had left him angry and bitter. Have you ever seen such a face?

To be angry is such an easy thing to do. It is so easy to get angry. Anyone can get angry, and of course everyone does get angry. But to be angry at the right person, to the right degree, at the right time, for the right reason, and in the right way — that's not an easy thing to do at all.[5]

Theologians through the ages have suggested several ways to deal with anger.

First, make an inventory of the things that make you angry. Identify those things or persons that make you angry, and then take steps to avoid them. Better yet, seek a way to be reconciled to them.

Second, make a vow to yourself that the next time your blood starts to boil you won't blow up. Promise yourself that the next time you will stay cool and talk quietly and reasonably.

Third, consider the other person's situation. Maybe you are just too fussy, too much into control, too prideful. Maybe what that person said or did that made you so angry was in fact helpful.

Fourth, you can avoid anger by being self-critical. Remember, no one is perfect; we all make mistakes. As the saying goes, if you never make a mistake, you never learn. We all need acceptance and healing. Be humble, be patient. The journey of life is too brief and full of enough potholes without your anger.

Fifth, when your anger button is pushed, start counting to prevent a blowup. Thomas Jefferson said, "When angry, count to ten before speaking, if very angry count to 100."[6] But then Mark Twain said, "When angry, count to four; when very angry, swear."[7] I think what Twain was referring to is what the character Raymond did in the movie *Rain Man*. Driving back to California Raymond learns that his business is going bankrupt, he owes $75,000, and some of his property has been confiscated. In a fit of anger he walks out into the desert and starts kicking dirt and rocks and swearing vehemently at his predicament. Then calmly he gets back into the car and continues heading west.

If you find yourself getting really angry, maybe you should follow Raymond's example: kick some dirt, kick a rock or a tree; only please don't kick the nearest person to you, or even the one who made you angry. Here a rule of thumb for parents seems in order. In raising children never punish your child when you have lost your temper. Punishing children usually does call for some degree of anger, but if you are in a blind rage, the punishment can be more violence than discipline. Get control of yourself. Counting before you lose your temper, or stepping back and away, can be very helpful.

Sixth, talk your way through anger. A frank but tactful approach to the person with whom you are angry, asking him why he said what he said, can lead to reconciliation.

Finally, number seven, if all else fails, say a prayer for the strength to give up your anger. Remember this: there are only two things you can do with anger: you can let anger eat at you like battery acid, spoiling your life or even destroying it; or you can give your anger over to God. "Vengeance is mine," says the Lord, "and I will repay." God is steadfast and works justice. God will repay and right the wrongs that are suffered. Our task, as followers of God and believers in God's mercy and judgment, is to give our anger over to God for God to handle it. Give your anger to God. You can't change the past, there's no way; but God can change the future, if you will only permit it.

Children's Message

For an object, take with you a mirror. Say to the children, "I want you to think of a really angry thought. Think of someone you're mad at, or of a time when you were treated mean and unfairly. Do you have it in your mind? You should be so mad now that you're frowning! *(Hold up the mirror for them to see their faces.)* How do you look and feel when you're mad? Does your face feel all crunched up, your stomach knotted up, your head tight? Now take a deep breath. Think about this beautiful day and your best friends. Put a smile on your face. Can you feel the difference? *(Show them their faces in the mirror.)* Now look in the mirror. They say that making an angry face takes a lot more work than making a smiling face. It is easier to smile than frown, isn't it? It feels a lot better to be happy than mad. God teaches us a lesson in this mirror. The Bible tells us, 'Don't let the sun go down on your anger' (Ephesians 4:26). In other words, get rid of your anger before you go to bed. It's just too hard and unhealthy for you. What God really wants us to do is have a smiling face. That's why God made it so much easier to make a smile."

---

1. Todd Jones, *op. cit.*, tape number 8.

2. Adapted from Jones, *ibid.*

3. See George Sinclair's sermon, "The Third Deadly Sin: Anger" (First Presbyterian Church, 120 Broad St, LaGrange, GA 30240), July 31, 1994.

4. I have adapted this list from Todd Jones, who adapted it from Les Carter's book, *Good 'n' Angry* (Baker Books: Kentwood, MI, 1983).

5. Jones, *ibid.*

6. Quoted in *The Living Pulpit*, "Anger," October - December 1993, Vol. 2, No. 4 (The Living Pulpit: Bronx, NY), p. 30.

7. *Ibid.*, p. 29.

Sloth

What Happens When Indifference Meets Enthusiasm?

Matthew 25:14-30; Revelation 3:15-16

A speaker at a revival, Edd Matney, spoke about commitment and motivation. When you think of commitment, Edd indicated, consider the egg and bacon on your breakfast plate: indeed, it took some commitment on the part of the chicken to lay the egg, but by comparison that was only a shadow of the commitment rendered by the pig to provide you your bacon. The chicken was involved, yes; but the pig was committed. In other words, are you involved or committed? Just how cold or hot are you as a Christian?[1]

Concerning motivation, think of the man who took a shortcut through a cemetery to his office early one morning. He fell into a freshly dug grave and couldn't get out. Along came another man who also fell into the same grave, but he didn't see the first man. After watching the second man try to get out, the first man finally spoke up, "Don't worry, someone will come along and help." Suddenly, on hearing a voice in the grave, the second leaped out of the grave and took off running. In other words, a voice motivated him to solve his problem. What voice motivates you? Two key words in the battle against sloth are commitment and motivation.[2]

Elie Wiesel tells the story of a young Jewish man named Michael who returns to his Hungarian hometown at the end of the Second World War. Michael had been imprisoned in a concentration camp but had survived the brutality. He returns to his hometown in Hungary out of curiosity, not for revenge. In particular he is curious about a man who lived across the street from the synagogue where Michael used to worship. This man watched from his window day after day as hundreds of people were herded to their deaths. This man watched with no pity, nor anger, without even pleasure or interest as people were marched to death. He just watched: impassive, indifferent, impersonal. It didn't matter to him one way or the other. He didn't care one way or the other.

In a strange way Michael understood the brutality of the guards and the executioners at the camp. At least their passion to inflict suffering and death was something that was part of the world. But the man behind the window, who looked and showed no passion nor interest whatsoever, was just a spectator. He didn't belong to the world. Evil is human, anger is human; to cause suffering is human, to express hatred is human; but indifference, to show no emotion, to be neither cold nor hot, that's inhuman. The man behind the window with his indifference commits the sin of sloth. Like the people of Laodicea, he is neither cold nor hot. He's just a spectator, lukewarm, worthy only for being spit out.[3]

Sometimes sloth is thought of as meaning laziness. In fact it is on account of what appears to be a lazy pace of life that a creature in the Amazon jungle was named the sloth. It moves so slow that it was viewed as a lazy creature.

A farmer was sitting on a porch one day, a piece of straw in his mouth, his feet on the railing. He was the picture of contentment and ease. A stranger came along and said, "Hello," and then asked him, "Anything new going on?" The farmer replied, "Well, yes, sir, there is. Two weeks ago a tornado came through here. The tornado cut down all the trees I thought I was going to have to cut for firewood. It was wonderful; it saved me a bunch of work." The stranger said, "That's incredible, anything else?" The farmer said, "Yes, last week we had a lightning storm and lightning hit a field of brush I thought I was going to have to cut. It burned the whole field down and saved me a whole week of hard labor." The stranger said, "That's amazing! With all that time and labor saved, what are you doing now?" And the farmer said, "I'm sitting here waiting for an earthquake, hoping it will throw those taters out of the ground that I have to harvest."[4]

Sometimes sloth is portrayed, like that farmer, as laziness. But you can also be a very active person and still commit the sin of sloth, because the essential meaning of sloth is not laziness. Sloth describes a lack of caring, an aimless indifference to God and others and even an indifference to your own life.[5] Even a person who is extremely active can commit the sin of sloth. You can be a booming success, or the model of a dedicated parent devoted to your children, and still be guilty of sloth.

Take for instance Albert Speer in his autobiography, *Inside the Third Reich*. In that book Speer confesses that he was so enthralled by the power of his position as Hitler's State Architect that he was blind to the slaughter that was going on around him. Albert Speer was a brilliant architect, a hard worker, a good husband, a wonderful parent, and one who certainly did not hate the Jewish people, in fact he said he greatly admired the Jewish people. But Speer confesses that his mind was set on his professional career, that he was so intent on doing his job that he was oblivious to the horrors going on around him. The name of this blindness is none other than sloth.

> *Sloth is the sin of being unconcerned about the world and people around us.*
> *Sloth is when a person turns his head away when he meets someone on the street who is in need or a victim of crime.*
> *Sloth is a person throwing pollutants into a stream or landfill or a company exposing people to toxic materials.*
> *Sloth is well-clothed and well-fed people ignoring the needs of the poor and the hungry.*
> *Sloth says, "I don't care."*[6]

The parable of the talents is a story about sloth. The parable describes a man who, immobilized by fear and a bad theology, buries his gifts. He was afraid that if he did do something he might fail. And the bad theology was that if he did try and yet failed, the Master would be angry. In the final analysis he just didn't care enough, he didn't have enough commitment and motivation in himself or in his Master, and so he didn't do anything. He was lukewarm. Jesus says then that such a person, being lukewarm, is cast out.

On another occasion Jesus said we are the salt of the world, but if we have lost our saltiness, then we are no longer good for anything. Jesus also said we are the light of the world, but if we hide our light under a bucket so that no one can see it, then again it is good for nothing. Lukewarm salt and lukewarm light; good for nothing.

As someone has said, "All it takes for evil to triumph is for good people to do nothing." That is, "All it takes for evil to triumph is for good people to be lukewarm." And so we have sloth.

Of course, good people have good excuses for their sloth. They say, "There's so much wrong in the world, I can't possibly do anything to help. I'm just one little person." But what in the world is one little person? Do you know that our county would cave in and dry up if just little people didn't care? The men and women who volunteer their time and talents to the hospital, to the civic clubs, to the schools, to the churches make a difference in this community. Every day they do battle against the forces of evil to help people and to make this a better place to live. And everyone of them is an unsung hero, just one little person, but one little person making a big difference in the world because he or she cares.

One of the most common symptoms of sloth occurs as we grow older. In the so-called midlife years and beyond, our goal in life is to "make something" of ourselves and "to make a difference."[7] In the middle and older years of life we look for ways to contribute to life. To have a successful business, maybe to raise good and decent children, to be a community helper. In the middle and older years of life we think about leaving behind a legacy, a good memory, and a good work. The danger though is that sloth will enter into our hearts and make us think that our lives have been for nothing, that we have not made something of ourselves, nor made a difference. If that happens, we will stop caring about ourselves and others, and life will lose its meaning and sense of direction.

The writer of Ecclesiastes seems to have reached that point when he said, "Life doesn't make sense; you toil and sweat and struggle; life is hard and all is vanity, and then you die." When you hear these words you have to say Ecclesiastes looks very lukewarm. He seems to throw up his hands and say, "I don't know about God, and I don't know about life." Lukewarm. Yet in the end he shows some heat when he finally concludes, "Fear God and keep his commandments." There at the end of all his moaning and complaining he recognizes, "I do have something meaningful to do because of my relationship with God."

This is all spelled out much better in the Book of Revelation when the angel speaking to the Laodiceans says, after they have been declared to be slothful, to be neither cold nor hot: "Listen! I am standing at the door, knocking; if you hear my voice and open the door, I will come in to you and eat with you, and you with me." In other words, the cure for sloth is a relationship with God. But it takes effort. You have to open the door. You have to take action.

As you would expect, the opposite of sloth is zeal or enthusiasm. Zeal, enthusiasm, means not just doing something because you have to, but doing it because it arises out of communion with God. Remember when Abraham was tested by God? "Abraham, take your son, your only son Isaac, whom you love, and go and offer him as a burnt offering." Abraham was a compassionate and just man. It was out of this compassion and sense of justice that Abraham pleaded with God to spare Sodom and Gomorrah, if only ten righteous people could be found living there. Abraham, as a man of compassion and justice, is one who would never willingly sacrifice a human being. But here was God demanding the sacrifice of Isaac: the promised child, born to Abraham and Sarah in their old age; precious Isaac, the one through whom God promised to make a great nation. Considering all that Isaac meant to Abraham, I would expect Abraham to procrastinate, to put off taking Isaac to the mountain to be sacrificed. But the Bible says that on the appointed day, Abraham "rose early in the morning" (Genesis 22:3), cut the wood for the sacrifice, saddled his horse, and set out with Isaac for the mountain. Abraham didn't delay; he was zealous, enthusiastic, to do the will of God.[8]

Perhaps you saw that special on the ABC television program *20/20* in which they interviewed a group of men and women who had reached the age of 100 or more and were still physically and mentally agile. There were three things in particular they had in common that seemed to help them reach that centennial mark.

First, they had a positive outlook on life. They had all been through the grief of losing parents, brothers and sisters, friends, and spouses, and yet they still had a positive outlook on life. They enjoyed life and enjoyed making new friends. They were thankful for the life they had, expressing no bitterness for anything in their life.

Second, they stayed active helping other people. One woman, 102 years old, acted as a volunteer tour guide for a historic home. Another woman over 100 years old led an aerobic class for what she called "whippersnappers in their seventies."

Third, they were believers in God. They believed God had a purpose for their lives, even if it were a small purpose. So while they were near the end of their lives, they still had a sense of meaning and purpose.

Zeal, enthusiasm, is that attitude of exuberance in which you know that many things are possible. Enthusiasm is a feeling of fervor. Communion with God means knowing and having this same attitude and fervor that many things are possible. To know God, to be in relationship and communion with God, gives us something to do that indeed makes a difference in life.

One particular way to experience zeal in life is to consider all the good things you enjoy and give thanks to God for them. All of us, no matter what our condition in life is, have some good for which we are grateful. The poor man has something to eat, some clothes to wear; and the sick person is still alive and surely has family and friends who pray for his or her recovery. The apostle Paul admonishes the Christians at Philippi to rejoice by thinking about whatever is true, whatever is honorable, whatever is just, pure, lovely, gracious, anything worthy of praise, think on it and rejoice (Philippians 4:4-8). This is not pie-in-the-sky gratitude. You can question the justice of God, and you can argue vehemently against God for suffering and pain as Job did, and yet at the same time have an appreciation for life that is able to sustain you in the worst of times.

Another weapon in the combat against sloth is to remember that every good deed makes a difference no matter how small it is. It is noteworthy to consider that every great journey is made up of one footstep at a time. Judaism and Christianity have always taught that to help one person is as if one helped the entire world; and conversely, whoever destroys one person is considered to have destroyed an entire world.[9]

Let me leave you with this image. Back in the days of slavery, life was grim for slaves. If anyone had a reason to despair of life and not care, it was the slaves. The work was long hours, hard and dirty. And after a full day's work, what did they have to show for it at the end of the day? Nothing. They were slaves; they had nothing of real value. When the slaves would come in from the fields at night with their dirty faces and ragged cloths and looked at each other they would cry with grief and despair. But when they looked up and remembered the Bible stories, then they sang and even danced the hopeful spiritual songs.[10] What I say to you then is this, "Rejoice!"

Children's Message

When someone comes to your house and knocks on the door *(make a knocking sound),* what do you do? That's right, you go and answer the door. You go and see who it is and if it's a friend, or someone you know, you invite him or her in.

The Bible says Jesus is knocking at the door *(again, make a knocking sound).* How do you let Jesus in? Well, maybe if you see someone who is hurt you could offer help *(making a knocking sound).* Or if someone at school is being picked on, treated badly, you could be his or her friend *(making a knocking sound).* Or maybe listening to a Sunday School story and looking it up in the Bible is a way of letting Jesus come into your heart *(make a knocking sound).* Or even worshiping God is a way of letting Jesus come in *(make a knocking sound).* Let's pray about this knocking.

---

1. The source for this illustration is unknown.

2. Norman Vincent Peale, *How To Handle Tough Times* (Foundation for Christian Living: Pawling, NY, 1990), pp. 23f.

3. See William White, *Fatal Attractions: Sermons on the Seven Deadly Sins* (Abingdon Press: Nashville, TN, 1992), pp. 41-42.

4. Todd Jones, *op. cit.*, tape number 2.

5. Schimmel, *op. cit.*, pp. 191, 193.

6. Adapted from White, *Fatal Attractions*, p. 43.

7. See George Sinclair's sermon, "The Fourth Deadly Sin: Sloth" (First Presbyterian Church: LaGrange, GA), and Donald Capps, *Deadly Sins and Saving Virtues* (Fortress Press: Philadelphia, PA, 1987), p. 58.

8. Schimmel, *ibid.*, p. 194.

9. *Ibid.*, p. 209.

10. From a sermon delivered by Ernest Campbell, Massanetta Springs "Bible Conference," Summer 1994.

Lust

To Discipline The Eye And The Heart

Matthew 5:27-30; John 4:5-26

Jesus and his disciples were in a foreign land, the land of Samaria. It had once been recognized as the birthplace and capital of the Jewish faith. It was in Samaria and at Shechem that God told Abraham that the land would belong to his descendants. But later the Israelites were defeated by the Assyrians, who then settled in the land and mixed with the population. So in Jesus' day the people of Israel viewed the Samaritans as half-breeds and false worshipers. Jesus' parable of the "good Samaritan" was a contradiction; to the Jews there were only bad, corrupted and devious Samaritans. To the Jews there was no such person as a "good Samaritan." For instance, while the Samaritans called the town Jesus stopped at by the old name of Shechem, meaning oak, the Jews called it Sychar, meaning drunkenness. Obviously, the Jews had only a bad opinion of the Samaritans.

Jesus was on his way back to Galilee and decided to take a shortcut through Samaria. A self-righteous, religious Jew would never have taken such a shortcut; instead, he would have taken the long way around Samaria. But Jesus took the shortcut right through Shechem. Being weary from the journey, Jesus decided to rest and get a drink from a well near the town. There, while he rested, a Samaritan woman also came to the well to draw water.

Her arrival at the well at that time tells a whole story. It was noontime, and normally water was drawn in the morning and the evening. Also, there was a well 300 yards closer to the city. Why was this woman here drawing water at this well at noontime? It soon becomes apparent in the conversation she has with Jesus. This woman has lived a promiscuous life of one affair after another. She had been through five husbands and was now living with yet another man who was not her husband. She had now come to draw water at noontime at this far-off well because the other women would not let her draw water from the closer, main village well at the normal times. She was an outcast.

When Jesus asked her for water this woman responded, "What? A Jew asking a Samaritan for water? Where have you been? Jews don't drink after Samaritans." And Jesus said, "If you only knew who was asking you for a drink, you would ask him for living water. Because everyone who drinks the water out of this well will be thirsty again, but those who drink the water I give will never be thirsty again."

Here was a woman who attempted to satisfy herself with a half dozen relationships and found each of them unfulfilling. Water is an appropriate symbol for lust. Those who are thirsty for sexual pleasure find that they are seldom satisfied.[1]

A lot of things come to mind when we raise the issue of lust: the advertising industry with its use of sex-appeal to sell us anything from cars to dishwashers. And the pornography industry which is doing a booming business. For instance, while you may not think of it as pornography as such, the swimsuit issue of *Sports Illustrated* is its biggest selling issue of the year, and it sells big not because of anything to do with baseball, football, or basketball.

There's the widespread and apparently common sexual harassment of women at work, and, yes, every now and then, even of men. Remember the Senate hearing of Supreme Court Judge Clarence Thomas and Anita Hill?

The music industry, both rock and roll and country/western, seems to thrive on the lyrics, "I want you, I need you, I love you!" as though all three meant the same thing, and of course they don't.

There's the promiscuity of Magic Johnson and others who contribute to the spread of the AIDS virus. There's O. J. Simpson, whose jealous lust made him into a violent spouse abuser.

People everywhere pay a terrible price for lust. "Lust is the parent of thousands of unwanted babies"[2] and of thousands of abortions. Lust is the hammer that breaks human hearts. Lust does away with people as having feelings, hopes, and dreams, and sees them as only so many body parts, or just a thing to have.

We heard the report of Susan Smith in Union, South Carolina, who did away with her two young children by driving them into a lake to drown. The reason? We don't know for sure, but she had received a letter from her boyfriend which said he was not ready to have a family. The murder of her children appears to have been partly due to lust; perhaps she thought she had to have that boyfriend at any price. If that's true, then we see and know how lust is not just a titillation of the eye, not just a fleeting thought, but that it can even kill.

The Bible of course recognizes the passion of sexual desire. The Song of Solomon or Song of Songs is all about the passion of sexual desire: "Love is strong ... Its flashes are flashes of fire, a raging flame." Throughout the history of the biblical faith this passion described here in the Song of Solomon has been played down. The Jews said it described God's love for Israel, and then the Christians said it described Christ's love for the Church. But of course it does neither; it portrays the passion of love between a man and a woman. In other words, the Bible testifies that the passion of sexual desire is a fact of life and blessed by God. When Adam first saw Eve he excitedly proclaimed, "This at last is flesh of my flesh." Or, as one of my seminary professors translated it, "Wow, she's the one all right!" But when sexual desire runs amuck, when a husband or wife finds himself or herself looking at someone other than his wife or her husband, and saying, "Wow, now that's the one!" then the deadly sin of lust has entered the heart.

We sometimes use the word "lust" for the word "covet." The basis for that is found in the Ten Commandments, where the tenth commandment tells us not to covet our neighbor's property or his wife. So covet and lust are sometimes interchanged. For instance, someone can say, "He's lusting after that red Corvette," or we hear the expression, she has "a lust for life" or "a lust for money." But this morning I will be using lust in the limited sense of referring to human sexual desire that is out of control, because that is what Jesus demands us to do in his description of the nature of adultery: to control ourselves.

The Bible, though, is not against human sexuality or even against the physical attraction between a man and a woman. Remember, the Bible quotes us Adam's remark on seeing Eve for the first time. Remember again, the Bible includes the Song of Solomon, a love letter depicting the passion between a man and a woman. In the Bible human attractiveness is not dirty, shameful, or lewd; the attraction between a man and a woman is a gift from God. God created us in his own image as male and female and pronounced it good. One could even say that the physical attraction between men and women incarnates our attraction for God. As we were created to be attracted to one another, so too we are attracted to God for the fulfillment of our lives.

But what the Bible opposes is the attraction that wants merely to use another person for gratification. It will help to think of lust in contrast to love:

> *Lust wants to get and take.*
> *Love though seeks to give and share.*
>
> *Lust seeks to dominate.*
> *Love seeks relationship.*
>
> *Lust uses the other person.*
> *Love seeks to enhance the other person.*
>
> *Lust treats the other person as an object, a thing to be used.*
> *Love, however, desires a personal encounter, the dignity and appreciation of the other person.*[3]

The kind of action lust displays is directly opposite to the action of love. All who pay attention to the dark shadows of their hearts know the distinction and can readily name it.

Perhaps you remember a few years ago how Jimmy Carter sent people back to read their Bibles, the fifth chapter of Matthew. Carter gave an interview with *Playboy* magazine while he was President. In the interview he said that while he had never committed adultery in a physical way, he admitted that he had lusted in his heart.

Carter knew what lust was in the biblical sense, and simply admitted publicly what is a common sin of the heart.

What Jesus tells us quite frankly makes common sense: adultery is indeed a problem of the heart and mind. As anyone knows, before you start mopping up the water on the floor, you first turn off the faucet. In the same way, you deal with adultery by turning to where the problem is, by turning to the heart and mind where it begins with lust.[4]

What Jesus tells us is that the sin of lust is not only what you do with your hands, your feet, or your eyes, but this sin is first of all an attitude of the heart and mind. So Jesus tells us that we have to discipline ourselves in how we look and think about others for whom we have a physical attraction. As Martin Luther said, "You can't keep the birds from flying over your head, but you can keep them from building nests in your hair."[5] What is called for is discipline and control. We are not like the leaves of the trees blown about by gusts of wind; we can and are able to control the ways of our hearts and minds.

Lust arises on the scene very much like envy. Perhaps you remember that a few weeks ago envy was described as a problem of thinking that the grass is greener on the other side? Lust causes the same thoughts. It makes us succumb to the big lie that "with her or him, it would be better." But would it really?

If you were to ask people who have lived to a ripe old age what they were looking for in life, I can almost guarantee you that 99 out of 100 will say, "I was looking for love." Among all the things we want in life what tops the list is our desire for relationships, to be loved and to love someone else, to share a life of hopes and dreams, to have companionship. In other words, what people are really looking for is the kind of sharing and commitment you find only in marriage; yes, in marriage with all the wrinkles, receding hairlines, and tummies needing to be tucked in.

So how do you discipline yourself to avoid the sin of lust? Jesus said, "If your right eye causes you to sin, pluck it out. If your right hand causes you to sin, cut it off. It is better to lose one member of your body than for your whole body to be defiled."

Everyone, of course, agrees that Jesus is exaggerating here. Jesus is not asking us to mutilate ourselves. He's not to be taken literally here, although there have been some in the history of the church who have, which resulted in the mutilation of themselves. Such actions totally miss the point of Jesus' teaching, because you can be totally blind and a double amputee and still commit the sin of lust. The problem is not in the eye or the hand; the problem is in the heart. Jesus is giving us an example, telling us exactly and graphically how important it is to be vigilant and self-disciplined about our attention to people to whom we might find ourselves strongly attracted.

One approach is simply to avoid that person or spend less time with him or her. In other words, instead of plucking your eye out, or cutting off your arm, remove that person from your eyesight, put some distance between you and that person. In place of seeing and being with this other person, spend more time with your wife or husband. You may even want to do something you haven't done in a long time — take your wife or husband out on a date!

Another approach is to get realistic: appearances, as we all know, can be deceiving. If you really knew some of the most beautiful people in the world you would find that they are not perfect and that they are incapable of making your life a "happy ever after" story. Like everyone else, so-called "beautiful people" have their physical ailments, irritating habits, hang-ups, drives and dreams. You might well find it very difficult to live with them. The chances are these people could not fit into your way of life, they could not enter into a vital, living relationship with you if you were realistic. In being realistic you ask yourself, what are you really looking for? Common sense will tell you that surface beauty doesn't equal a meaningful relationship for sharing life in all its dimensions.

Todd Jones, a friend of mine from my student days, describes the time when his mother received word that the lump in her breast was malignant and had spread to the lymph nodes. A radical mastectomy was required and performed. After the surgery Todd recounted that the entire family was gathered together in his mother's hospital room to discuss the possibility and procedure for rebuilding the breast that was removed. Todd says he will never forget what his father said to him that day. His father had been married to his mother for over forty years. Taking him to the side, his father said, "Todd, your mother is beautiful to me no matter what she looks like on the outside."[6] You see, there is a vast difference between love and lust. Love is the real thing that lasts and makes life possible, while lust is fleeting, shallow, having no true substance.

Finally, what you can do to overcome lust is to confess it to God. "Lord, look at me. This is how I feel, these are my thoughts and fantasies. Release them from me and let me remember who I am and to whom I belong."

Remember that Samaritan woman at the well? It is important to note that Jesus didn't condemn her lustful life. No, he didn't condemn her; instead he offered her a new way of living. He called her to drink living water, he called her to confess her sin and repent. And she accepted the offer, made her confession and turned around. Where she was once thirsty for more than water and was not satisfied, she could now say: "Come, see the one who quenched my thirst."[7] Come, indeed, to Jesus Christ and follow his way. Be disciplined in the matters of your heart, and be satisfied.

Children's Message

Do you have boyfriends and girlfriends at school? Are notes passed between boys and girls at school? *(Give a note to a boy and a girl. Have them, or help them, read it aloud. Both notes have the same message: "I think you're nice.")* It's only natural for boys and girls to be interested in each other. God made us that way. The Bible says God made us in God's image. God made us male and female, boys and girls. God said it was good. God meant for boys and girls to be friends. Of course, I know you boys sometimes think the girls are too mushy. I know you girls sometimes think the boys are too mean. But not all the boys are too mean and not all the girls too mushy. You can and do find boyfriends and girlfriends who are really fun to be with. It's good to have boyfriends and girlfriends. And remember this, Jesus is also your friend, and a friend to others, too. The Bible says it's good to have friends; it's good to have boyfriends and girlfriends.

1. White, *Fatal Attractions*, p. 60.

2. *Ibid.*, p. 61.

3. Adapted from Todd Jones, *op. cit.*, tape number 7.

4. W. Clyde Tilley, *The Surpassing Righteousness: Evangelism and Ethics in the Sermon on the Mount* (Smythe & Helwys Publishing: Greenville, SC, 1992), p. 88.

5. Quoted by Tilley, *ibid.*, p. 89.

6. Adapted from Todd Jones, *ibid.*

7. White, *Fatal Attractions*, p. 63.

Greed

Putting Things In
Their Proper Perspective

Matthew 6:25-34; 1 Timothy 6:6-10; Ecclesiastes 5:10-11

Mr. Jones had a job that gave him a comfortable income. He enjoyed fishing and motorhome camping. Every year or so he would buy a new combination fish and ski boat, not some little dinghy, but a really nice, fancy boat. Every couple of years Mr. Jones would buy a new motorhome camper. It was obvious that several other men in the neighborhood envied Mr. Jones and tried to keep up with his new toys. They too would buy and sell boats and campers. It was obvious that keeping up with Mr. Jones was a priority in their lives. It's sad though, because such a priority means that you end up thinking that who you are, your value as a person, is determined by how much you have.

Lee Atwater, a political strategist under President Bush, died from a brain tumor at the age of 41 in 1991.[1] Reflecting on his life just before his death, he said, "The '80s were about acquiring — acquiring wealth, power, prestige. I know. I acquired more wealth, power, and prestige than most people ever dream of. But you can acquire all you want and still feel empty. What power I wouldn't trade for a little more time with my family."

I wonder what Mr. Atwater would say about a recent bumper sticker that said: "The one who dies with the most toys wins." My guess is he would say, "It's all wrong. It's a terrible lie."

Greed. Greed is never satisfied with "that's enough." No, greed says more is always better, because you can never have enough. Greed sees life not as a gift from God, but as a race to acquire, to get more, to have a bigger house, a bigger bank account, a fancier car, a bigger career position. Greed means we have to accumulate as much as we can, have more exciting vacations, more luxurious clothing. But with greed, as Mr. Atwater learned, "You can acquire all you want and still feel empty."

But greed is not just a matter of accumulating things. Greed is also a matter of people being bored with their lives. Nowadays people seem to think everything is so boring, so many people are dissatisfied with life. People sit in front of their television sets, flicking through all the channels with their remote controls, trying to find something that will entertain them because they are bored. In response to all this boredom, people try to fill up their lives with more and more: more exciting vacations, more expensive cars with all the extras, bigger homes. Like an additive drug, it takes more and more to get the same feeling of euphoria and security. More and more, bigger and bigger is needed.

I suppose it is true that everyone suffers from some form of greed. It is found not only among the rich, but also among the poor. In both groups you can hear it said, "If I only had 10,000 more dollars, everything would be alright."

Derrick Coleman, at the time a member of the New Jersey Nets basketball team, was offered seventy million dollars over nine years; that is, about 8 million dollars a year. Can you imagine? Of course it is money paid to keep us entertained, to keep us from being bored. His agent though responded by saying, "We really appreciate the offer, but we want to go after some really big money."[2]

In the face of that goal of going after "some really big money," the apostle Paul says, the love of money is the root of much evil. Now Paul didn't say *money* is the root of much evil, he said the *love* of money is the root of all evil. What he meant was that the love, or the consuming desire for money creates evil people. Why? Paul may have been reflecting on Jesus' comment that you can't serve money and God. In his letter to Timothy, Paul said that those who wanted more and more money didn't stay long in the church. In Paul's experience, he saw that the love for money created people who would do almost anything to have more and more, and let no one stand in their way, not friends, not family, not even God.

Of course, the craving for money is encouraged, supported, and promoted everywhere. Interestingly, it is illegal to be addicted to marijuana, cocaine, heroin, and other drugs. But addiction to television, shopping malls, outlet stores and the lottery is considered acceptable behavior as well as encouraged.[3] For a number of years the M.B.A. students at Duke University were asked to write out their personal life plans. The question posed to them was, "What do you want to be when you grow up?" With very few exceptions, they wanted three things: money, power, and things — and very big things, like vacation homes, expensive European cars, yachts, and airplanes. Their primary concern was the growth of their financial portfolios. Their personal goals in life very seldom included family, intellectual development, spiritual growth, or social responsibility.[4]

Our craving for things and more things is not like other cravings in the world. For instance, if you have a craving for food you can join a club like "Weight Watchers" that will help you to stop eating. If you have an alcohol craving, you can join an "AA" club to beat the habit. But have you ever heard of a club to stop your craving for money? No! Because there's not one. Instead, there's just the opposite kind of clubs, ones which help you gain more by buying in bulk, but none to overcome compulsive buying. There aren't even any books to help you overcome the compulsion to have more, such as, *How to Stop Your Craving for Money.*

Greed promises us a full and happy life. How many times have you heard it said, "If I only had more, life would be better." But as Mr. Atwater said, "You can acquire all you want and still feel empty." Think of a hand glove. By itself the glove is limp and lifeless; it can't pick up anything. But slide your hand into it and it acquires the power to do all kinds of things. Money is like a glove which by itself is neither good nor bad, but put it into the hands of a person and it becomes a personality. Money in somebody's hand can create a grasping hand or a giving hand.[5]

Perhaps you've noticed that greed starts early in life. It seems a child is taught that he or she never has enough toys, and that some other child has more or better toys. That's what our children learn when we buy them toys for every occasion. Early in life we learn to say, "I want that," and "That's mine!" Early in life we are taught that having things will make us happier. But will it?

Having possessions is not the problem. We all need possessions. Jesus said, "Your heavenly Father knows that you need all these things," such as food, shelter, and clothing. But greed is having our needs met and yet never being satisfied. So you have people who have incurred enormous credit card debts because they have come to believe that in order to be happy you have to buy. As the bumper sticker says, they are "born to shop." They have to have, and yet they never have enough.

The miser represents another kind of greed. The miser is eager to have by saving. Have you ever known someone who could never throw anything away? I have some familiarity with this one firsthand; just come and see my basement. Perhaps you know someone who saves everything: aluminum foil from packages, newspapers, odds and ends of all kinds. Why are these things saved? Not because he or she is environmentally aware about overflowing landfills, but because he or she is worried about not having enough. For the miser greed means our possessions possess us.

Another kind of greed is seen in the gambler. This kind of greed lives off the idea that you can get rich quick. The lottery is funded by this idea. It promises us riches, and all it takes is a few dollars. You only have to hear about a few people winning big, and you can get hooked into thinking, "I could be the next winner." All those millions of dollars just sitting there for you to win. You think of all you could have with all those millions — greed.

Every day we are bombarded with the idea that there are only two goals in life: one, to be successful; and two, to feel good. And the way to be a success and feel good is to have more and more. But is having more and more really good?

Perhaps the ancient Greeks had it right. They minted their money in heavy iron disks, rather than silver coins, to remind people that wealth is a burden. At the beginning of this century the average American had 72 wants and thought that 18 of them were essential. At the end of this century, the average American has 496 wants and thinks that 96 of them are essential for happiness.[6] That's a sixfold increase. To satisfy this craving for more, we have in this country twice as many shopping centers as we do high schools. People complain if taxes are raised to educate our children for the well-being of the future, but if a new shopping center is constructed no one complains; quite the contrary, it's welcomed as another opportunity to have greater access to more and more things. What has happened here? We have bought into the myth that as long as I have a chance to get more, life is better.

An elderly couple owned a picturesque 75-acre island in British Columbia. They needed to sell it and move to the city. It was a gorgeous island with the natural beauty of large trees, meadows, deep coves. This island would be ideal for yachts and multi-million dollar homes situated on hillsides with panoramic vistas. In fact, this couple was offered thirteen million dollars by a developer for the island. But can you believe it, they said no. They were not holding out for some really big money like Derrick Coleman. No, what they were holding out for was to make the island into a natural preserve. They asked the Canadian government what it would pay for the island. The government said it would pay three million dollars. That meant a loss of ten million dollars. But this couple wanted to leave behind something for everyone to enjoy; they wanted to leave a heritage. As it happened, the Canadian government didn't have the money to buy the island, but this couple persisted and found a group to buy it for three million dollars, preserving its natural beauty as an undeveloped public park.

What would you have done in their place? Would you have gone for the thirteen million dollars, land development and luxury homes, or settled for three million dollars and a nature park? An interesting question, isn't it? Indeed, imagine what you could do with ten million extra dollars. But could you live without it and live on only three million dollars? (Everyone is supposed to shake heads "Yes.") Indeed, everyone could say, "Hey, sure, I could live on three million dollars." Could you live on one million dollars, if it meant you could leave a heritage to your children and others? How about half a million, or 100,000 or even 20,000 dollars? Could you live on that if you could leave behind a heritage to your children and others? "What do you mean? Of course I could. I do it everyday." My question here, then, is this: is making and having money everything?

People tend to see life as two ways of living. "Having" is one way of living. This way of living means you have a job, a career in order to have things. Such a life is without a doubt important and necessary. "Having" is a way of accomplishing something in the world which is visible and tangible in things. On the other hand, there's the spiritual way of life. Here you pray for meaning in life through values that are tangible in terms of loving others, helping others to have food, shelter, and work. But you don't really have anything to show for this spiritual level. At the spiritual level you don't have things as such. And yet, if you ask the average person, it is matters of the heart that are the most valuable things in the world.

When a house catches fire, what is it above all that people will risk their lives to save from the flames? Their good china? No. Their Hummel collection? No. A family heirloom such as a great-grandmother's clock? Well maybe. But what people really seek to save in a house fire are the family pictures of the children, parents, grandparents — those things of the heart.

Jesus didn't divide the world into two ways of life, into a material and spiritual realm. Jesus said the way we think about having things impacts who we are, and what we do with our lives affects the very meaning of our lives.[7] Jesus gets at this by saying, "Where your treasure is, there your heart will be also" (Luke 12:34).

Jesus accepted and counted among his followers people who had many possessions, that is, wealthy people. Lazarus, the one whom Jesus brought back to life, was one of his wealthy friends, and so was Zacchaeus. Jesus accepted their hospitality and friendship. But Jesus was critical of anyone who thought the value of life could be measured by how much he or she had. He told a parable about a man who built more and more barns to hold his wealth, warning us to be rich to God. The question every day is this: "Will I strive to value my life on what I have, or will I strive to value my life on who I am as one who belongs to God?"

A family had a teenage son who had an accident while snow skiing. Apparently he had lost control on the slope and hit his head on a boulder, causing severe brain damage. He was in a coma for about three months. One day while traveling with his father to the hospital to visit his son, his father said, "You spend your life working to advance your career, to make a decent salary, to do the kinds of things that will make your life secure; and then suddenly you're reminded that the most important thing in life are the people in your life." Here was someone who was in effect saying, "It's matters of the heart; it's your relationship with other people that is most valuable and meaningful in life, and not how much you have."

How then do you overcome greed? One thing to do is to reflect on some of the biblical passages dealing with greed. Think about what Jesus said when he declared that, "Wherever your treasure is, there your heart will be also." Elsewhere Jesus said, "Give to anyone who asks you, and if anyone takes what belongs to you, do not demand it back" (Luke 6:30). And again Jesus said, "Do not be anxious about your life, what you will eat, or drink, or your clothing. Life is more than food or clothing. Your heavenly Father knows your needs" (Matthew 6:25). Reflecting on passages like these can help us put into perspective that while God intends for us to work and to enjoy the things of life, enough is enough.

Erma Bombeck, the columnist who delighted us with her humorous outlook on life, battled cancer. At one point in her writing career, Erma wrote a book about children with cancer, *I Want to Grow Hair, I Want to Grow Up, I Want to Go to Boise*. Erma found strength and encouragement in the comments and insights of those children.

She said that one little voice that constantly echoed in her mind and heart was that of eight-year-old Christina. Christina had cancer of the nervous system. On her eighth birthday she was asked what she wanted for her birthday. Christina thought for a long time; finally, she said, "I don't know. I have two sticker books and a Cabbage Patch doll. I have everything!"[8] For young Christina, in the face of losing everything, she said, enough is enough.

Another helpful thing to do to combat greed is to develop a contrary attitude toward having more and more. I remember getting a phone call: "How would like to double your income in the next year and become financially independent in five years?" I replied by saying, "I'm sorry, that really wouldn't interest me." The response on the other end of the phone was dead silence. Why?

Because you are supposed to be greedy and jump at any opportunity to have more and more. I wasn't interested for a very basic reason. Whatever the plan was for this get-rich-quick scheme, I knew I would have to change my lifestyle and commitments, maybe even my job and where I live. I knew also I would have to give my body and soul to the company making this offer. And that just wasn't me. I simply couldn't see my life defined in terms of this once-in-a-lifetime deal.[9]

Another contrary attitude is to be more generous in giving your money to various causes. We are taught from childhood how to make, how to save, and then how to spend money. But Jesus taught us how to give money. Making, saving, and spending money appeal to our greed. Yet knowing how to give balances the greed to make, to save, and to spend. It is by learning to give that we are spiritually nurtured.[10]

My office is full of books. I need books and I have a substantial investment in these books. One day a woman came to me and asked if she could borrow one of my books to do a Sunday school lesson. I said, "Yes, of course, and feel free to underline any important sentences and make notes in the margins. Make use of the book to get at the subject, although I wouldn't want any pages cut out of it." She then replied, "Are you serious? I was always taught not to write in books. I can't imagine writing in someone else's book." I responded, "Well, the way I look at it, this is my book, I own it, it doesn't own me. If I can only get it to help me by marking in it, then I do that, and I'm giving you permission to use this book as I do. Write in it all you want to, if it's helpful. Your marks in fact may help me to see something in it I've overlooked!" It is the same way with money or anything else we have. It is for our use. We possess it; don't let it possess us.

Finally, it helps to remember that you can't take it with you. As the apostle Paul says, we are born into the world with nothing, and when we die, we take nothing with us. Paul however does say that there is something we do take with us: the good things we have done in the name of Jesus Christ. As Jesus said, "Seek the kingdom of God and his righteousness." It is not in satisfying your craving to have more and more that you have abundant life. No, it is in serving God and loving others as you love yourself that abundant life is gained and lived.

Children's Message

(Show the children an advertisement for toys and ask if there are any toys they see that they would like to have.) Do you have a lot of toys at home? Why do you need another toy? *(The children will give various answers.)* Well, let me ask you a question. Would you rather have a toy that can break or leak or run down, or would you rather have a friend who, with a little special care, can play with you, stick with you, and have fun with you for a long time? I would rather have a friend, wouldn't you? Having friends to share your toys with is really the best fun. We are now in church, not to play with toys, but to learn how Jesus is our friend, and how we can be a friend to others. It's so good to have friends and to be a friend. It really is the best thing.

---

1. Lee Atwater, "Lee Atwater's Last Campaign" in *Life* (February 1991).

2. Quoted by Todd Jones, tape #4.

3. Thomas H. Naylor, William H. Willimon, Magdalena R. Naylor, *The Search for Meaning* (Abingdon Press: Nashville, TN, 1994), p. 74.

4. *Ibid.*, p. 10.

5. Herb Miller, *Money Isn't Everything: What Jesus Said About the Spiritual Power of Money* (Discipleship Resources: Nashville, TN, 1994), p. 6.

6. *Ibid.*, p. 5.

7. *Ibid.*, p. 2.

8. *In Other Words...*, edited by Raymond McHenry (Houston, TX), Vol. 5, Sept/Oct. 1995, Issue 5, p. 3; drawn from *Reader's Digest*, April 1993, pp. 96-98.

9. Adapted from Tom Eisenman, *Temptations Men Face* (InterVarsity Press: Downers Grove, IL, 1990), p. 155.

10. See Eisenman, *ibid.*, p. 155f.

Gluttony

Living By Bread
And The Word Of God

Mark 6:38-42; 1 Timothy 4:4-10

Every day at about 10:30 in the morning and then about 3:30 in the afternoon, I need a little snack to keep me going. A cookie or some pretzels, some quick and easy snack to get rid of a growling stomach; something to give me a boost so I can get my work done. If I go too long without some snack food, I get to feeling run down. I even become grumpy and irritable. Then I can't do my work because I'm thinking about food.

Eating food is, of course, a necessity of life. We need food to live, to do our work; we even need food to be sociable, likeable people. Have you ever tried to eat with someone you didn't like or with whom you were angry? You can't do it! It is like eating stones and with a stomach twisted up in knots. Food is not just protein, vitamins and minerals; eating food is a way of living.

In the novel *Zorba the Greek*, Alexis Zorba asks his young friend, the boss, "Tell me what you do with the food you eat, and I'll tell you who you are. Some turn their food into fat and manure, some into work and good humor, and others, I'm told, into God."[1]

Food. "Tell me what you do with the food you eat." Food occupies a major portion of our lives. With all the time spent on buying, preparing, eating, and cleaning up, not to mention the snacks, food is a major preoccupation in our lives. It should come as no surprise then to hear that more people struggle with food than you might ever imagine. Also, more people have problems with eating too much than may be apparent. As a case in point, a recent poll indicated that two out of three people consider themselves overweight.

Gluttony is a major problem in this country. I'm not speaking here about a theology of dieting. The sin of gluttony is not about good or poor eating habits. Gluttony is not about overeating, or even about being overweight. Instead, gluttony is about making food such a central concern in our lives that the time we spend thinking about food and dealing with food pushes other more important matters aside. Another way to put this is that all of us who are overweight are not necessarily gluttons. A painfully thin, anoretic teenage girl who engages in cycles of self-starvation and eating binges has her life almost totally dominated by food; and such a life is one of gluttony. Seen in this way, undereating can be as much of a problem as overeating. The sin of gluttony is making food into a god; food is allowed to define who we are and is looked at as a way to solve or relieve the burden of our problems.

Naturally all of us experience the necessity to be diligent about not overeating and the necessity to be diligent about what we eat. Yet this is how the problem of gluttony arises: we have to think about eating food. Such thinking can become a struggle, and a particularly difficult struggle for us Americans because we are bombarded by food on all sides. Nearly every street corner has some kind of food available for us. You are never anywhere far from food. In addition to all that, the variety of food in the grocery stores is staggering.

The problem is compounded for us because we are bombarded every day by messages in the newspaper and on television about food and drink. Curiously though, while we get all these messages to eat more in the newspaper and on television, we are also told by the very same media that bone-skinny is beautiful. So we are given a double message that centers on food. In addition, our children are given the message that food is the way to be happy. On Saturday morning the commercials for kids' cartoons are not predominantly about toys; they're predominantly about food: cereals and fast foods. "Here children, eat this, and you'll be happy."

Gluttony is ranked as a deadly sin because food can be seen as a way to make us feel happy. Eating can become a way for us to avoid or solve our problems. You can use food to divert your attention away from problems, instead of trusting in God and taking up a life of responsibility for your problems. Again, as in so many things, the problem is not the food itself; the problem is in the way we misuse food to numb ourselves to our problems, misusing food to fill our emptiness, looking to food to satisfy our loneliness.

One reason food becomes misused is due to the amount of time we devote to it. If you were to count the amount of time you spend thinking about food, shopping for food, preparing food, eating food, and cleaning up afterwards, you might be amazed at how much time it amounts to. For the average person it amounts to about twenty percent of the day. In other words, in every 24-hour period you give five hours to food. For some people it can be anywhere from forty percent to seventy percent of the day. And for a foodaholic it can be as much as eighty percent. Any way you look at it, those are not small numbers.[2]

To cut down on the amount of time consumed by food a lot of families eat out. Another Gallup poll indicates that the average family eats forty percent of its meals out of the home, while some families eat as much as seventy percent of their meals outside of the home. In fact, for some families so many meals are eaten outside of the home that when Mom or Dad says, "It's time to eat," the children run to the closet to get their coats![3]

Certainly eating out can save on the time needed to buy food, prepare the food and clean up after the meal, but too often the kinds of foods eaten outside the home are fried foods high in fats and desserts high in sugars. Such foods cater more to a food-fix, producing a sedative effect on us and giving us a euphoric feeling. With such an effect and feeling, a cycle of food dependency can develop. When food is then approached for this purpose, it can all too easily become a way to make us feel good and solve our problems. But whether we eat in or eat out, when food is used to make us feel better, feel happier, and numb the burden of our problems, it becomes a tranquilizer and even a god.

Eating food is a necessity of life. You have to eat in order to live, it's not optional equipment for living. Thus food becomes a means to express the way we live. The Bible itself knows this because it has always looked to food as a way to express our relationship with God. When God promised the Israelites the Promised

Land, God said it would be a land "flowing with milk and honey"; in other words, a land abundant in food ready to eat. The Israelites responded, saying, "Let's go."

Food has played a major role in the history of God's relationship with us. Isn't it interesting to note that eating food was the reason Adam and Eve were cast out of Paradise? The first sin concerned the desire to eat.

Later, Esau sold his birthright to Jacob for a bowl of bean soup. And then Jacob received Esau's blessings by tricking his father Isaac over a pot of stew.

Israel was sustained in the wilderness with manna and quail, but then the people rebelled against God because of the food they remembered eating in Egypt: the melons, the vegetables, the roasted meats. They turned against God over food.

The Old Testament prophets spoke out against those who were well fed, while outside their doors the poor went hungry. Food was the occasion for the judgment of God.

In the New Testament, when Jesus talked about life in heaven he often described it as being a great banquet where you joined with others to eat. There was also the scandal that Jesus himself ate with sinners, which was a sign that for anyone whose life is empty God will fill it with grace, acceptance, and meaning.

Finally Jesus gave us a memorial to remind us of who he is and what his life was about, in the breaking of bread and in drinking from the cup. In the history of biblical faith, in the story of our own faith, the eating of food has been a sign of our relationship with God. Two aspects of eating food have played a prominent role in expressing that relationship: fasting and feasting.

The act of fasting is a particularly important expression in the Bible in our relationship with God. Most people probably think of fasting as starving yourself to misery. But fasting is about focusing on God and the things of God. If you decide to fast, remember that it doesn't mean starving yourself. During a fast you can eat small portions of fruit, maybe a small bowl of chicken broth, maybe half a sandwich. In the Sermon on the Mount, Jesus talked about being blessed, he talked about a deeper expression of the Law, he talked about prayer and taught us how to pray, he talked about giving money to the poor, and finally he talked about fasting as part of being one of his followers.

In the Bible fasting is always related to prayer because it helps us to focus on God by disciplining our bodies, our minds, and our spirits. In fasting you can give your full attention to the person who is in need. Just consider the request you make for someone to pray for you, or when someone says to you, "I'll pray for you"; such statements become more than just nice words when fasting is involved.

I once had an illness and a woman came and said to me that she was fasting for me. Such an action on my behalf had a powerful and humbling effect on me. Someone was really spiritually connected to me. Why is it that we so easily follow Christ's discipline to pray for one another but don't follow his example of fasting for one another? We gather together on Wednesday evening for Soup and Sandwiches and then have a prayer meeting conducted with full stomachs. Maybe we ought to skip the food, gather for prayer, and then go home and continue our fasting.

Such a suggestion may not be well received. I was once a member of a men's civic club that met on Monday evenings, beginning with a pot luck meal provided by the women of the local churches. As it happened, one November I was placed on the food committee to arrange for the meals. Being a minister and always having to do something "meaningful," I decided that we should have a meal that would remind us that in the midst of all the food of Thanksgiving there are men, women, and children who go to bed hungry every day. So that Monday before Thanksgiving I served bowls of beans and white bread.

When the men arrived, expecting a lavish meal but seeing only bowls of bean soup and bread, more than several were irritated. In fact, some were angry. Needless to say, I was never put back on the meal committee. One man made this comment: "You should have given us a lavish meal and then told us of the plight of hungry people. I give better from a full and guilty stomach." That was an interesting comment in light of the fact that Christ himself often gave to others from an empty and guiltless stomach.

There is a time to fast, but there is also a time to feast. Jesus encouraged us to fast so we could focus our attention on God. But Jesus also encouraged us to feast so we could focus on God. As far as we know, Jesus never refused an invitation to a meal. He would go and eat with the most self-righteous, hypocritical people in town one night, and then the next night he could be found eating with the worst of sinners in town. In fact, all this eating earned Jesus the reputation of being a glutton and a drunkard. But you see, Jesus knew that in eating with people you share yourself and God's blessings. Eating with others is a time of close communion.

Remember what happened to the disciples at the inn in Emmaus? They were sitting there at the table, and when the bread was broken, their eyes were opened and they recognized the Lord in their midst. Eating food with others is a time of communion, a holy time when we are nourished not only physically but spiritually.

When we celebrate Thanksgiving in our churches and in our homes, it will be a time of sharing food with others in joy and conversation. Thanksgiving was originally meant, and still is meant, to be a time of feasting to focus on God. It will almost be like communion in church, as we gather to remember and give thanks for the bounty we enjoy from God. There is a time to fast, and there is a time to feast. But we look neither to the food of our fasting nor to the food of our feasting for abundant life; we look instead to God who alone is the power of life abundant.

Children's Message

When my family and I sit down to eat we always say a prayer. We say our mealtime prayer by putting our hands together like this. *(Show the children the traditional way of praying with open hands held together.)* We pray like this to tell God that we are thankful for the food we are going to eat. Our mealtime prayers remind us that God gives us life.

Now take a look at this table here. It's like a dining room table, a table for eating food off of. We call it the table of our Lord's Supper. On special Sundays we have on this table bread and a cup of juice, and everyone here is allowed to share that bread and that cup. The bread and cup help us to remember that God gives us life, and so we're very thankful. It's like a time for prayer, but instead of holding our hands together, we open our hands to receive the bread and the cup. Receiving from this table, we remember all of God's promises to us, and our promise to follow God and do the things Jesus teaches us.

---

1. Quoted by White, *Fatal Attractions*, p. 80.

2. See Schimmel, *op. cit.*, p. 140.

3. Todd Jones, *op. cit.*, tape number 5.

www.ingramcontent.com/pod-product-compliance
Lightning Source LLC
Chambersburg PA
CBHW071747040426
42446CB00012B/2491